CONFESSIONS OF A YAKUZA

A Life in Japan's Underworld

JUNICHI SAGA

Translated by JOHN BESTER
Illustrated by Susumu Saga

KODANSHA INTERNATIONAL
Tokyo • New York • London

Originally published by Chikuma Shobo in 1989 under the title
Asakusa bakuto ichidai. Previously published as The Gambler's Tale.

Distributed in the United States by Kodansha America, Inc., 575
Lexington Avenue, New York, N.Y. 10022, and in the United Kingdom
and continental Europe by Kodansha Europe Ltd., Tavern Quay, Rope
Street, London SE16 7TX. Published by Kodansha International Ltd.,
17-14 Otowa 1-chome, Bunkyo-ku Tokyo 112-8652, and Kodansha
America, Inc.

ISBN 4-7700-1948-3

www.thejapanpage.com

Contents

III

IV

Acknowledgments

The original edition of this work was published with the help of Kazama Motoharu, of Chikuma Shobo, to whom I am deeply grateful. The English version has been indebted at every stage to Stephen Shaw of Kodansha International, who with his wife Toyomi showed a constant interest in the work from the outset, recommending even before the Japanese version had appeared that it should be translated into English. I am grateful, too, to the translator, John Bester. That he should have chosen this work from among so many possible candidates for translation says something, I feel, about the peculiar fascination of Ijichi Eiji's world—a world apparently alien from Japanese norms, yet revealing in fact so much of the average man's thoughts and feelings.

Translator's Note

All Japanese names in the text are given in the Japanese order: family name first. A number of cuts have been made in the original, with the author's permission, in order to eliminate passages that would be perplexing or tedious to the non-Japanese reader. I am particularly grateful to the editor, Stephen Shaw, for his excellent work in tightening up and enlivening the translation.

I

It was a winter's day, several years ago. An elderly man, tall and solid-shouldered, turned up at my clinic in Tsuchiura, a town about an hour away from Tokyo by train. His face was a good deal larger than the average person's, with a forehead deeply lined with dark creases, thick, purplish lips, and a muddy, yellowish tinge to the eyeballs: the kind of face that at first glance set him apart from most people.

I got him to strip to the waist. His whole back was covered with a tattoo—a dragon-and-peony design, though the colors had faded with the years, leaving the dragon's scales pale, like stylized clouds, and its whiskers almost at vanishing point. Even so, the design was striking and, in its way, oddly attractive. Inside the petals of the peony stood a woman. The dragon was about to swallow up the peony, and the woman with it. Her eyes were half-closed and her palms joined in prayer, but an enigmatic smile played around her lips.

I would have liked to photograph it if possible, but I'd never seen the man before in my life, and something about his air of absolute assurance made me hesitate, so in the end I never got around to making the suggestion.

Examining his abdomen, I found the liver enlarged. It was obvious that there was fluid collected in the abdominal cavity. As I waited for him to get up from the examining table, I said,

"I'll give you an introduction to a general hospital; I think you'd better get treated there."

But he smiled slightly and said,

"I'm seventy-three, doctor. I've done pretty much as I pleased all my life, and I don't expect to be cured at this stage."

The inside of his mouth was black with nicotine, so that it was like peering into a small cave. His voice was low and hoarse.

"I was a bit wild when I was young, I'm afraid, and now my body refuses to do as I say any more. So I decided to hand the gambling place over to one of my younger men and retire here to the country. You know the massage woman who lives below the embankment? I had her give me a rubdown two or three times; quite a hand at it, she is. She was the one who recommended me to come to you."

"I see."

"I'm not going to get better, whoever treats me, am I?"

"Did they tell you that at some hospital or other?"

"I can tell myself. To be honest, I didn't come here with any high hopes. I just thought maybe you could give me a shot sometimes when it hurt. Now, don't worry—I'm not asking for drugs or anything. I expect it's because of the diabetes, but my legs hurt like hell at times. I thought perhaps you'd take a look at me then, and make things a bit easier."

Since he seemed unwilling to accept any fuller treatment, I decided to do what I could to help. I had my own reasons, though, for agreeing to this arrangement. I see dozens of different people every day in the course of my work, but I'd never come across anyone like this man

4

before. There was something intriguing about him. And privately I decided to get him to tell me all about himself someday.

He began to come to my clinic twice a week. Fortunately, the abdominal fluid didn't increase as much as I'd thought it might, and the pain in his legs, too, continued for a while to give him little real discomfort. Then, one day about a month later, he asked me if I'd care to go and see him at his place when I had the time.

"It's just a shack, I'm afraid," he said, "but I can manage a cup of tea and a warm place to tuck your feet in. I imagine you've had a normal, decent sort of life, so it might be interesting for once to hear about something a bit different."

Early the next evening, in a cold, driving rain, I went to visit the man at his house. He was waiting for me, with a pile of mandarin oranges in a bowl on the small table covering the sunken hearth, ready for his guest. Occasionally, the faint sound of someone playing a samisen was audible through the drumming of the rain.

"It's the girl amusing herself," he explained.

As to whether it was his daughter, though, or how old she was, he told me nothing. That evening, I listened to him for about three hours. Every thirty minutes or so he seemed to get tired, and we would take a break for a cup of tea; politely, he would invite me to take one of the mandarins, then peel one carefully for himself and eat it before proceeding in his hoarse voice with the next short section of his tale.

In this way I came to visit him, with a tape recorder, at least once every three days. And by the time I had more or less heard him out, the cold winter had slipped away and spring breezes were blowing across the land.

What follows is a part of his story as he told it to me. Now I come to set it down, I find myself wishing that I had questioned him more closely about all kinds of things; but he is gone, and it is too late now.

5

Oyoshi

I was fifteen when things first started to go wrong.

His voice was quiet as he began to talk, but he spoke carefully, so there was no problem catching what he said.

My father at the time owned one of the best general stores in Utsunomiya, selling salt and sugar, fabrics, bedding, and so on. The farmers from the country round about used to come pulling handcarts and buy everything they needed there, from ordinary household things to gifts for people on special occasions. He must have had at least fifteen employees; the young assistants would be dashing around among the piles of goods, and the clerks clicking away at their abacuses. We used to give our best customers their midday meal in a separate room; the maids kept a great pot of rice going for the purpose. It's years ago now, but I can see it all as if it was just the other day.

Anyway, the money rolled in, and we lived in style. My old man was fond of buying watches. He'd have them sent from Tokyo, and kept a whole bunch of them on show in a special corner. Then, at the summer Bon festival and New Year's, he'd give them out to clerks and assistants who'd been working well. It was different then from now, watches weren't to be had for the asking, and these were gold watches into the bargain, Swiss-made, so they were worth a fair amount. My old man would sit there like a feudal lord, with his back to some fancy flower arrangement. The staff would be sitting in front of him, red-faced from bowing down till their foreheads touched the floor. When the chief clerk called out a name, the man who was to get the watch would come crawling up on all fours, and my dad would say "You've worked hard" or something of the kind, then he'd hand over the watch, taking his time about it. The younger lads used to get so excited they'd shake all over—you could tell at a glance how pleased they were. I reckon he carried on with this routine just for the pleasure of seeing their faces.

My dad had a big house and garden just outside the town, which his parents used. Around the time when I first went to middle school, he had an extra house built to rent out at the back of the garden. When I say "to rent out," you mightn't think it was anything much, but it was a big two-story place, decently built, with its own entrance hall and an alcove for flower arrangements in the best room at the back. This house I live in here is two-storied too, but it's a shoddy affair compared with that one. Houses in those days were almost all one-story. The only exceptions were local government offices, schools, and so on, so an ordinary house that had a second floor was something pretty special.... Anyway, when I was in fourth grade at middle school, a young woman came to live there. She was the mistress of the chief judge in Utsunomiya, barely over twenty and, as I remember, very pretty.

My earliest memory of her was one day in autumn. I was coming in at the back gate when I saw this woman I didn't know looking out of an upstairs window. She had her hair done up in one of the traditional styles, all black and glossy, and was leaning on the rail outside the window, with her left hand up to her forehead and her right hand dangling outside the railing. It looked just like something in an old woodblock print. I stood watching her for a long time from behind a tree, wondering why someone like her should be there. After a while, my father came out of the front entrance, with a well-dressed fellow right behind him. He was showing him around, talking too much all the time and bobbing his head up and down. He wasn't much of a one for making up to people, and it was the first time I'd ever seen him behave like that.

The young woman joined them outside and said something to her well-dressed friend, who just nodded and grunted. For some reason this really turned me off him.

That was the day the judge came to look at the house; the woman herself moved in about ten days later.

It was always on a Sunday, in the daytime, that the judge came to visit her, never on a weekday, not even Saturday. He used to turn up in a rickshaw. He was a stout, imposing-looking man somewhere around his mid-forties. He'd climb down from the rickshaw in his formal kimono, wearing wooden clogs and carrying a cane; and while he was standing there, the woman would have a quick word with the driver and give him a tip.

The judge stayed with her till it began to get dark, when the rickshaw came to fetch him again, with a paper lantern hanging on one of its shafts. As he moved off along the dark road, leaning against the cushions, the girl used to watch him go.

I had to go to the woman's place once every month to collect the rent. Being a tradesman, my father couldn't live in a good residential area himself. My younger sister and my mother lived with him over at the shop, but I myself was with my grandparents, who were living in retirement there in the suburbs.

So it was my job to get the monthly rent and take it to my father's place. As she handed the money over, the woman would just say, "Here you are, thank you." I never heard another word from her until one day in winter, toward evening. When I arrived for the rent and stepped into the hall, her voice came from the other side of the paper sliding doors: "Come on up, Eiji."

I didn't say anything, so a door opened, and there she was, sitting in the sunken hearth with a pair of chopsticks in her hand.

"I'm just toasting some rice cakes. Do you want some? Don't just stand there—come on inside! Come and get warm. Come on, get in!... Tell me—how old are you?"

"Why?"

"It doesn't matter. Just tell me."

She looked me full in the face, smiling slightly. Then she picked up a rice cake that she'd just toasted in her dainty fingers.

"Now, open your mouth...," she said.

The white fingers flashed in front of my eyes, I felt dizzy and couldn't breathe properly.... And that was when my life started to come unstuck.

I went completely overboard, as you can probably guess. The woman was lonely, and I was fifteen at the time, so everything apart from her stopped existing for me. So far, my grades at school had been among the best, but now they suddenly crashed to somewhere near the bottom of the class.

When I was with her, I was always horribly on edge, my heart pounding with fright at the idea that the judge might turn up at any moment. I actually thought that if I was caught in the act there, a policeman would come for me and I'd be put in jail—sentenced to death, maybe.

This made her laugh, and she'd tease me about it: "If it bothers you so much," she'd say, "why don't you just shove off? The only thing is, if you do, I won't let you in here tomorrow or ever again." All it took was one tug on the leash and she knew I'd come trotting back to her.

Oyoshi

There were a couple of things, though, that bothered *her* as well: the judge's wife and the big house they lived in. I used to pass the house on my way to school. It had a moat about six feet wide all the way around it—just like a castle. On the far side of the moat was a thorny hedge and a wall, to stop people getting in. A pine tree in a tub stood on each side of the front door.

Inside the entrance hall there was a big step-up made of a single piece of wood. There was always a rickshaw waiting to one side of the entrance, with a man sitting next to it. They had a tennis court on the east side of the grounds. This was in the 1910s, mind you, and I'd never seen *anyone* playing tennis in a country town like that. Socially, a judge in those days was really something; he ranked alongside the prefectural governor, so I expect this one wanted a residence to match his position.

But it wasn't so much the house as the wife inside it that made her ask me all about it when I got home.

I remember a little thing that happened once. It was an early evening in summer with a hot wind blowing, and the woman, who'd had a bath, was lying on the tatami in the living room in nothing but a shift. I'd just got out of the bath myself too; I came into the room with nothing on but a loincloth and the steam rising all over me. All of a sudden, the girl chucked her fan down on the floor.

"She's an awful nag," she said. "She's always going on at him. Like this—" She made a kind of frown between her eyebrows with her two forefingers.

I wondered who she meant.

"His wife!" she said bad-temperedly, picking up the fan again and fanning herself for all she was worth.

"I wish she'd just hurry up and die," she added.

"You ever met her?" I asked.

"Oh, yes! Just the one time. He took me to the Kabuki once when I was still in Tokyo, and his wife and daughter were in the next seats. The daughter was about the same age as me."

"That's a funny thing to do, isn't it?" I said.

"Funny? Ridiculous, I call it!"

She may really have been hoping the wife would die. But even if this had happened, there was no guarantee at all that she would have stepped into her shoes—which was another thing that made her fret. The judge had rented a house for her and gave her everything she wanted, but it didn't seem to satisfy her. It made my blood boil when I saw her like that. I don't know why, exactly—I was just furious.

Then, one evening near the end of summer, I was sitting there with my mind blank, trying to think of something to do about it but getting nowhere. Outside the window was one of

11

those little bells that tinkle in the breeze in summer. I was looking at it when suddenly I felt I couldn't stand things any longer. So I pulled the bell off its string and slammed it down on the paving stones outside in the garden.

"What's up with *you*?" she said. "You scared the life out of me." She glared at me as if she found the sight of me disgusting.

"What's it matter to you?"

"Oh, cut it out!"

"I'm asking you."

"Don't be stupid!"

She took my chin in her fingers and twisted it sharply, then smiled brightly. Then she looked straight into my eyes and said it again, in a whisper: "You're stupid," she said, "like all the rest of them!"

Well, the same sort of thing went on for I don't know how many months, till the woman suddenly upped and ran off to Tokyo. The judge had been shifted to a better post, and she was moving so as to be with him. When we said goodbye, she said she'd write after she got to Tokyo, so I was to be sure to go and see her there. But I waited and waited, and it was three months before a letter came—then when it did, it didn't have any address on it.

It must have been about six months later that I went to Tokyo myself. My one aim was to see the woman—I had this idea that so long as I got there I was bound to meet her somewhere. When I told my father I wanted to find work in Tokyo, he agreed with surprisingly little fuss. Seems he felt it wouldn't be a bad thing for me at that point to depend on someone else for a change. I mean, I was in fourth grade at middle school, but it was obvious I wasn't going to pass my exams. In those days, it was normal to fail students who didn't do their work, so he probably thought it would do me good to find some way to support myself away from home.

"However tough things get, though, don't come here complaining." Those were his parting words; I don't expect he had any inkling of why I wanted to go. The young woman's first name was Oyoshi—it's funny, but I don't remember ever hearing her surname.

Fukagawa

A cousin of my father's was a coal merchant at Ishijima-cho in the Fukagawa district of Tokyo; the firm called itself the Nakagawa Coal Depot. That's the place that took me on.

The man stuffed some chopped tobacco into the tiny bowl of his long-stemmed pipe, lit it, and puffed at it in a leisurely way. He gazed at the burning charcoal in the brazier, the hand that held the pipe trembling slightly, so that the brownish bowl swayed to and fro.

It was quite a big business in its way. Outside the office there were dozens of heaps of coal piled up way over your head, stuff that they'd bought in places like Hokkaido and Kyushu.

When a ship carrying coal arrived in Yokohama, laborers would reload it onto wooden barges. These would be drawn by tugboats up and into the Sumida river, then from Mannen bridge they'd come down the Onagi river and along between the rows of factories and shops till they reached our depot. The depot had five wharves on the riverbank. The laborers then piled the coal up in the storage yard, ready to be shifted onto other boats or horse-drawn carts as soon as we had an order from some firm.

They were a really scruffy lot, you know, the laborers. Apart from anything else, they were filthy. The skin on their faces was all dry, their teeth were yellow, and they had a mean look in their eyes. I asked my uncle once why they all had that look, and you know what he said? "Because they're scum."

My uncle was rich, but he was stingy. He was always warning me to be careful how I recorded the amounts of coal the laborers had carried. "Rough estimates are no good," he'd

14

say. "They make a tremendous difference one way or the other in the long run, so you've got to record everything exactly." He had a small moustache and always wore a cloth cap, with a broad-shouldered jacket and riding breeches, plus high leather boots. He kept a cloth in his pocket which he used to wipe the boots with whenever they got dirty.

He was incredibly fussy about details. "Those laborers," he'd say, "—their one idea is to slack off whenever you're not looking. But just think what that means to us: if a man carries two pounds less every time than he says he does, that means a loss of a hundredweight on fifty trips. Or a loss of five tons if there are a hundred men. That's why you've absolutely got to keep a sharp eye on the scales."

I soon got fed up with him harping on the subject, and only half listened to anything he said.

Though I'd come to Tokyo hoping to meet the woman, I didn't know my way around at all, and on top of that I was worked off my feet, so there just wasn't time to go and look for her. My first job, as I just mentioned, was to jot down in a ledger how much coal the laborers carried. The amount for one trip was fixed at a hundred and thirty pounds. If we were loading a boat, they'd use hods to lug it over to the edge of the wharf, where I'd be waiting with a pair of scales.

"Come on, get a move on!" I'd say. And I'd get the usual answer:

"This is as fast as a man can manage!"

I'd draw a line by the laborer's name and hand him a bamboo stick. These sticks were called *mambo*, they were about a foot long and an inch thick. The laborer would hold it in his hand as he trotted up the gangway. Then he'd dump his coal down anyhow and hand over his *mambo* to another youngster like me waiting on board, who'd also put a mark by the man's name.

15

So my work brought me into close contact with these men. When you got to know them, most of them were OK. They tended to fly off the handle easily because they were always hungry, but they were basically nice enough. As I was the youngest at the site, they'd often ask me how old I was, or if I wasn't going to school. And one of the old hands kept a friendly eye on me, so I soon began to feel more at home.

It was about two months after I started working there that I was asked to act as a lookout when they were gambling. I'd noticed that at the midday break all the laborers went off somewhere, and I'd assumed they'd gone to have something to eat. But that didn't quite seem to fit, so I decided to poke around among the coal heaps. As there were thirty or forty of these heaps in the storage yard, each of them as high as a two- or three-story building, it was like walking through a maze. I pressed ahead, though, and came across a lot of men squatting down in a ring. When they caught sight of me, they jumped up with a yell, and some of them started running. Then, when they realized it was only me, they suddenly looked relieved. "Come on," one of them said, "it's only Eiji." This was a young lad known as "Balloon" Shinkichi. He had a wrinkled forehead like an old man, and he got his nickname because he looked as if his head had been pumped up with air.

"Look, stay away from here," he said. "Just shove off, and don't go telling the boss or anybody about it, either. Here —this is for you." And he gave me two sen.

Just then the foreman strolled over and said, "Eiji—come over here for a second," and he took me to the base of the biggest coal heap in the yard.

"I want you to get up on top of that pile and keep a lookout. If anybody comes, let us know."

"What for?" I said.

"You should know what for—if the police caught us we'd all be locked up. You're not to come down till I tell you to. If you see anything fishy, chuck down a piece of coal."

"I might hit somebody on the head."

"Don't worry about that."

"What do you mean by something fishy?"

"You'll know soon enough when it happens. But don't go calling out—just chuck a piece of coal."

I did as I was told and climbed up to the top of the heap. It turned out to be a terrific height, higher than anything else around. At that time, even in Tokyo, about the only tall buildings were factories, so there was a good view in every direction.

Anyway, I got through that day without any trouble and acted as a lookout the next day too. It made me take a real fancy to the old districts of Tokyo, looking at them like that from way up there. There were boats moving up and down the rivers and canals, making this steady drone that drifted up into the sky, and mixed in with it you could hear the railway and people's voices and carts and other sounds. Listening to them gave you the feeling you were really in a big city, and I felt pleased with myself. I went on keeping watch for them, but luckily we were never caught by the cops, and I never once had to throw any coal.

I even went to another gambling place on my own once. It was on a converted barge tied up alongside a jetty. They used it as a bathhouse, too. Below decks they'd made a bathtub, and the families of the boatmen round about came there for a good soak. Obviously, they had all the water they could use, and they made do with floating wood for fuel. There was no partition or anything between the gambling area and the bath, so the women and children took their clothes off right in front of you before getting in. And they'd sit there soaking, with their towels on their heads, watching the men play. It was summer, so the doors were left open, and you could see the moon reflected on the surface of the river.

I'd been collecting the bamboo sticks for about half a year when my uncle told me I was to switch over to delivering coke, which we also dealt in. It was cheaper and easier to use than charcoal, so most of the smithies and ironworks in Tsu-kishima were using it. The whole area was full of these little workshops—one man working a foot bellows to get the coke burning bright red, and three or four others hammering away at the red-hot iron from morning to night, turning out pots, stoves, nails, farm tools, and building materials.

Carrying my ledger and briefcase, I had to go with the carts on their rounds, collect the cash, and hand over the receipt. My uncle seemed to trust me with the money, and was only worried that I'd lose the briefcase. If it was a small delivery, we used a handcart, with one guy pushing and another pulling; a lot of the time I went with two laborers in particular: "Balloon" Shinkichi and "Soldier" Tarokichi.

Tarokichi had fought against the Russians—he'd got a medal to prove it, but he'd pawned it before I got to know him. Shinkichi, though, had been a tenant farmer until five years or so before. He told me he'd often come to our part of the city to get nightsoil for his fields.

"You know, I used to be able to tell just what kind of food a family was eating," he said. "At a house where they ate well, the shit was different—it was richer, had more *body* to it. The color was different, too. You could tell right away."

"So the rich and the poor even shit differently, eh?"

"One time, though—it makes me feel a fool just to remember it—I got in an awful mess."

"What kind of mess?"

"I upset a bucket of the stuff right in front of a restaurant—next door to the second-hand clothes shop by the canal, it was. They made a hell of a fuss, so I hadn't much choice, I tried scooping it up with my hands and putting it back in the bucket, but that wasn't good enough, so I took off my kimono and used that to get it up with. When it got full I washed it in the canal then started all over again, I did it any number of times, and in the end I was all covered with the stuff. I jumped in the canal to get myself clean, but—I mean, it was October—it was freezing! And all those goddamn people standing around watching, with funny looks on their faces because they didn't know whether to laugh or complain about the stink."

"That must have been a sight!"

"You're telling me. At any rate, at least I know what they mean now when they tell you to 'eat shit.' "

In the days when I was carting coke around with Shinkichi, the nightsoil men were a common sight. A lot of them came by boat if they didn't live nearby. You'd see them going around calling out "Nightsoil, nightsoil!" in the alleys, with a long pole on one shoulder and a bucket dangling on each end. If anyone indoors shouted "Nightsoil maaaaan!" they'd go to the little trapdoor on the outside of the house by the toilet, poke their pole inside with a scoop on one end, and draw the stuff up. When the buckets were full, they'd take them back to their cart, then hang a new set of buckets on the pole and set off again. And by the time they'd stowed a few cartloads of full buckets on board their boat—they slept there, too, when it got dark—the job was done and they sailed away.

The Pox

Getting on for a year after I was given the job in Fukagawa, a guy called Shinji—he worked at a shop making the rubber-soled socks that workmen used to wear—took me with him to the red-light district. He was fond of gambling, and whenever he had time to spare he'd turn up at the coal yard and lose some money before going home again. That particular day, though—I don't know what came over him—he was in luck and won some money, so he said to me, "It's on me today, so just keep quiet and come along."

Shinji's idea was that once in a while I ought to get my hands on something else besides coke: all work and no play, as they say ...

"A man should sow plenty of wild oats while he's still young," he said. "Get a whiff of the boudoir. Have some nice mature woman show you the ropes...." He was only just over twenty, though from his face you'd have thought he was past thirty.

He used to sing as he walked along. Silly songs, like:

> He swaggers by—my former beau—
> In best kimono dressed,
> A pocketful of cash to go
> On women and the rest.
> I never will forget him—no,
> Where'er he comes to rest!

But the place he took me to wasn't one of the classier brothels, it was a cheap teahouse along the alley leading up to the Hachiman shrine. The real business of that kind of teahouse was to provide women, so they didn't do any fancy food—only dumplings, sweet saké, rice crackers, cakes, and tea to go with them, at the most.

"Is she free?" Shinji asked the proprietor, shoving a dumpling into his mouth.

"Yes, sure."

"It's not for me today, it's for this youngster here. Look after him, will you?"

The proprietor took me farther down the alley, where there were lots of small houses all jammed together any old how. We walked a way, then came to a house with a ginkgo tree in front of it. We went through a wooden gate in the fence and into the garden, where there was a separate cottage at the back.

"Hey—I've brought you a customer!" he called out.

"OK," came a woman's voice, so we opened the front door. Inside there was a poky little hall space; the sliding doors were wide open, and beyond them a young woman was sitting on a quilt, spread on the tatami.

"Well! He's young, isn't he? What a nice surprise."

"Here you are, then, I'll leave him to you. But don't go thinking it's all right to tire yourself out for the rest of the day, just because he's young."

"Oh, get out of here—you talk too much!"

She turned to me and said sweetly, "Come on in. How old are you?"

I was putty, of course, in the hands of somebody like her. I mean, I wasn't seventeen yet and the woman was obviously well over twenty, so she must have been a real veteran. When she undid her sash, she didn't have anything on under the shift she was wearing, not even a waistcloth. She just sat there with it open at the front, inviting me. She might as well have pinned me down by the back of the neck—she couldn't have done better if she'd tried.

You know, I can't remember her name however much I try. All I know is that I hadn't been in bed with her all that long when someone started tapping on the front door, scaring the daylights out of me.

"That's enough—I can hear you!" the woman yelled. "Is it time already?"

"You've had exactly thirty minutes."

"So what?"

"You've got another customer. Can I open the door?"

"Not likely! Who is it, this customer? A regular?"

"No, it's the gentleman's first time."

"Well, shit—what about me? I'm human, too. Why can't I take my time with a decent-looking man once in a while? Tell him to wait!"

"He's here with me now."

"Oh, go to hell! What d'you take me for? How many customers am I supposed to take? At this rate I'll be dead before long."

"It was thirty minutes, wasn't it?"

"Don't ask me—it was *you* fixed it, wasn't it?"

All the time she was shouting angrily like this, she still had hold of me. I tried to make her let go.

"I'm off," I said. "I feel bad about it."

"No you don't!" she said. "Don't worry about *him*—he's making a fortune as it is." And she wrapped herself around me like a snake.

"You can have him wait over at the shop," she called out again.

"How long will you be?" the boss snapped back.

"Half an hour."

"D'you think he can wait that long?"

"The dirty old man—if he doesn't like it he can fuck off!"
She wasn't going to let anyone get the better of *her*.

The upshot of all this was that I took a kind of fancy to the
woman. And I visited the place about three times altogether.
At first I thought I'd really fallen for her, but then I suddenly
took against her. For some reason or other she started turning me off, and I stopped going. Just like that.

I've known a lot of women in my life, but the thing about
the professionals was that they were fairly cut-and-dried—they
didn't come chasing after you when you got tired of them. So
they were convenient if you were just out for a good time.

That reminds me of something else. The owner of a cheap
teahouse like that was also a kind of police informer. There
were two quite separate sides to his business, the legal and the
undercover, so if the cops wanted to get awkward they could
make it impossible for him to carry on. So whatever he did,
he had to take care to make up to the local policeman. When
it got to around lunchtime, he'd get the maid to make a bowl
of pork on rice or something and have it ready. Then the cop
would drop in with an official "wanted" notice in his hand to
ask if anyone "answering that description" had been there.

"Well, officer—hard at it as usual," the proprietor would
start. "Now, let me see ... no, I'm afraid I haven't seen anyone
like this around. But anyway, you must be tired, why don't you
come in and have a cup of tea at least?"

He'd pour him what was supposed to be tea out of his little
teapot. But it would be saké—he'd have a pot full of saké
ready for such occasions, you see. They'd be at the back of the
shop, so it would look like tea to the other customers. Then
he'd produce a meal.

The copper would say "I really shouldn't let you do this," or something of the kind, but he'd dig in just the same, with a satisfied look on his face. Then, when he'd finished, he'd say "Well, then, if anybody suspicious drops in, let me know at once, will you?" And he'd take himself off.

The owner was actually rather proud of his connection with the police. Sometimes he'd appoint himself a sort of private detective, and make reports to them.

"If you ask me, officer," he'd say, "this man who's always coming to see Oharu at our place acts a bit suspicious. Something tells me he's got a pile of money he didn't come by honestly. Perhaps you'd better keep an eye on him."

"I see...," the policeman would say. "Well, then, the next time he turns up, have the maid let me know immediately."

Then, the next time the man appeared, the teahouse owner would secretly send someone to inform the police. Of course, they'd never barge in on the man while he was actually with a woman. They wouldn't arrest him inside the shop, either. They'd wait till he'd left and gone far enough for it not to cause trouble for the teahouse, and for the man not to realize that the owner had snitched on him, then they'd hail him: "Hey, you—come over here a minute, will you?"

They'd go through everything he had on him. And they'd ask him his address, his job, how much he earned, the names of the people he went around with—far more detail than with a routine checkup on someone's background. So if a man was up to anything at all fishy, they'd be onto it in no time. Personally I was never caught at the teahouse itself, but I was often stopped for questioning in the street, so I know from experience just what the local cops were like.

Things didn't last long, as I said, with the woman at the

teahouse, and only a month or so after that I took up with someone called Oyone. There are some things in connection with her that I'm not likely to forget in a hurry, so I'd better tell you about it....

Next to my uncle's firm lived a carpenter called Kyuzo. He was a regular at the dice games in the coal yard. His missus was a dark little woman with slanting eyes who was always on the go. She worked as though she was desperate—maybe if she'd given herself a break, the thought of her husband's bad habits would have been too much for her.

Anyway, they had six children, so they were poor. The children were always hungry; whenever Kyuzo sat himself down for a drink of saké, they'd all come and sit around him. They'd watch him drink, wide-eyed, sucking in their cheeks and giving great gulps from time to time. If there was, say, a bit of pickled radish to go with the saké, their mouths would come open as they watched him chew it, and you could see spit trickling down their chins.

Sometimes he'd say, "D'you want some?" And they'd all nod together, more like a row of puppets than human beings. So Kyuzo would pick up one slice of radish and give it to the oldest boy, who was about ten. The boy would bite off half and give it to the next oldest. Then he'd give it to the third one, who'd bite off half of what was left, and so it went on till by the time it reached the fifth kid there'd be less than the tip of your little finger left. So the smallest kids would start bawling.

"That's enough of that," he'd say, but it wouldn't stop them. So he'd give them another piece, this time starting with the smallest. But then, as like as not, that kid would eat the whole piece himself, and there'd be a fine old fuss. Poor Kyuzo couldn't even have a drink in peace. On days when he didn't have any work, he'd usually turn up at the gambling place, to work off his frustration.

Every day when it wasn't actually raining, Kyuzo's wife would be doing some washing. It wasn't the family's clothes: it was the underwear of the local whores and the cotton kimonos they kept for their customers. The red-light districts produced a tremendous amount of washing every day, so it was farmed out to women outside.

An alley in Asakusa

There was a woman they called the Boss, a kind of supervisor; every day she'd load the dirty clothes the brothels had given her onto a cart and go around distributing the stuff to the washerwomen, who'd wash it at so many sen apiece and deliver it to the Boss by nightfall. That was the kind of work Kyuzo's wife did, so she was always outside the house with her laundryboard and her tub. And there'd be another woman with her, helping her with the tarts' clothes. Oyone, her name was; she was under twenty, and quite a charmer.

When they'd finished the laundry the women would hang it up to dry in a corner of the coal yard, which was my uncle's property, so they were always quite polite to me, as if they had me to thank for letting them use the space. Before long, I began to take a liking to them—and in that way I gradually struck up a friendship with Oyone.

She was the daughter of a barge owner, and lived alone with her elder sister in a two-story house near us. Her parents lived on the barge; with seven children on board as well, the place had got so crowded that the two oldest girls had moved out and rented a room on the second floor of a shop selling fertilizers.

One day, though, there was a fire at the house next door, and the place where Oyone and her sister lodged caught fire too. This was in the middle of the night, but I was woken up by the shouts of "Fire!" and rushed out to have a look. I found the whole area ablaze—and there was Oyone, who for some reason hadn't got out in time, clinging to the roof and crying and screaming for all she was worth.

Burning flakes were drifting down all around her, and she was certain to be burned to death unless she did something pretty quick. Her elder sister, who'd managed to escape, was screaming at her: "Jump, Oyone! *Jump!*" with her hair all hanging loose. But Oyone must have been too scared, anyway she couldn't move. The whole place was in a complete panic, with people rushing around through the bits of drifting fire, all of them shouting like mad. I was wondering desperately what to do when I saw a big old-fashioned umbrella lying at the side of the alley.

It gave me an idea. I picked it up. "Here—use this to jump down with!" I shouted, and chucked it up at Oyone. If I'd thought about it calmly, I should have known that an umbrella wasn't going to be any use, but that's the kind of thing you do when you're in a panic, isn't it?

Anyway, I had this idea that it would save her. So I threw it up toward her, but I was in such a state that I threw it handle first, so that the umbrella opened up almost immediately and didn't get as far as the second floor. I finally got the hang of it, and flung it again with all my might. Oyone grabbed hold of it and jumped with it gripped in her hand, still unopened.

Till then she'd been paralyzed with fright, but the moment she got hold of the umbrella, her strength somehow returned, and she just shut her eyes and jumped. So she was saved. And we were lovers from then on.

Oyone's father was called Ichizo, and as it happened *he* was a great gambler, too. Sometimes he played with the laborers, but when he played with the boatmen it was always inside the boat.

His barge had a cabin about twenty square feet big, but that was where his wife and children stayed, so they set up a big thing like a tent on the deck where the cargo was piled, and played inside it, out of sight.

The police must have known about it, though, as there were raids once or twice a year at least. You should have seen the players when they turned up—they all dived into the river, like so many frogs—they'd be in the air almost before the lookout gave the warning. If somebody had called out "Police" as a joke, I expect they'd have jumped in without bothering to find out if it was true or not.

Anyway, Ichizo was a good-looking guy, in a hard sort of way, and quite a favorite with the women. Thanks to that, his wife got jealous. She gradually got more and more turned in on herself, and in the end she began to mess around with magic, praying to the fox-god and that kind of stuff. You'd often hear her mumbling what sounded like Buddhist prayers. This went on all the time Ichizo was out on the town. She'd be inside their boat, but you could hear it across the river and way into the distance. The river was always jammed with boats, but you could tell at once which one was Ichizo's.

One day, I went to the barge with Oyone just as Ichizo was coming home. It was early evening, in summer, and the sky was still red over in the west.

He grinned at us and said, "That's right—you have a good time while you're still young," so I suppose he was in a good mood. But then I saw that Otoshi, his wife, was standing bolt upright in the body of the boat glaring at him. Her face wasn't normal. She was all tense around the eyes and her mouth was drawn up at the corners, so that she really looked a bit like a fox herself. And she said in this spooky kind of voice: "Ichizo! You've been with that Tamayo from the tea-house again, haven't you?"

Ichizo didn't pay her any attention. He went on board and headed for the cabin, but his wife shoved him back and shouted in this weird, high voice, "A while ago the two of you went into the noodle shop by the Fudo shrine in Tomioka, didn't you?"

"Bullshit," muttered Ichizo, not to be drawn out.

"You both ordered tempura noodles there, didn't you?"

"What the hell are you talking about, woman?"

"But you found a fly in Tamayo's noodles when they brought them, didn't you? So you bawled them out and the owner apologized and brought you a new bowl and gave you ten sen back, didn't he?"

Ichizo just stood there looking startled; his face was all

30

pulled out of shape. And then, with us watching him, he grabbed hold of an iron kettle that was on the deck. "Take this, you old fox," he yelled and flung it at her head. My girl gave a shriek, but almost before she got it out, the kettle had hit Otoshi full in the face. There was a terrific clang, and then—you'd hardly believe it, but the kettle split clean in two and fell on the deck. Otoshi stood with her eyes wide open and her face all tight and pinched like a fox still. Ichizo didn't move, he was so shocked; then he suddenly went limp and plumped down on the floor.

It was completely dark by now, and there were lights on some of the boats. After a while, Ichizo picked himself up and went into the cabin, but he was laid up for the next three days with a fever.

Of course, that didn't mean that he gave up playing around. But he must have got scared of going out with Tamayo, because he seems to have dropped her in a hurry. They didn't throw the broken kettle away, they kept it as it was. It still beats me how something like that could have happened.

Talking of fox's curses, there was another thing, too. I'd been going with Oyone for barely three months or so when I began to get fevers from time to time. I was wondering what was the matter, but then I got this pain in the crotch, and the glands there started to swell up. Even so, I thought it would clear up of its own accord and didn't do anything about it.

But it got more and more painful, till I couldn't even walk properly. If my kimono so much as touched my thighs, I'd jump with the pain. The laborers all cackled when they saw me walking about with bandy legs. After a while, though, I wasn't even walking—I was flat on my back in bed, with a high fever and my whole body shaking like a leaf.

It must have dawned on my uncle that this wasn't an ordinary fever, because he went and fetched the doctor. The doctor took one look and said "Syphilis." My uncle was furious.

"I didn't think you were such a slob!" he said. "I've a good mind to send you back to your father. What women have you been with, to get like this?"

"I haven't been with any women—it just happened," I said.

"You get syphilis having sex with women—who ever heard of somebody getting it by himself?"

He had a point, but I couldn't believe I'd got it from Oyone. She was such a clean and decent girl, you just couldn't imagine her with that kind of disease. Most likely it was the woman at the teahouse who gave it to me. But if so, I might have passed it on to Oyone. If I had, it would be awful. The idea really bothered me....

Anyway, the medicine and injections brought the fever down so that I was able to get up, but the swellings in my crotch went on getting bigger till they were as big as hens' eggs. They were incredibly painful; if I touched them by mistake, the pain just froze my brain.

"You'll have to get a specialist to look at this," my uncle grumbled. So I was taken to see a VD specialist in Kawagoe. My uncle got Kyuzo to go with me.

What surprised me was that when we went in at the gate, there were so many patients they were spilling outside from the entrance hall. All of them men. I don't know what they were doing to him, but you could hear a man screaming inside. It made my skin crawl. This is one hell of a place they've brought me to, I thought.

When my turn came and I went in, an elderly doctor with a beard had a look at me, and I was whisked onto an operating table right away. Three great brutes of assistants wound a leather belt around me, then lay down on top of me to hold me down.

"Listen—this is going to hurt a bit, but you're not to move, d'you hear?" the doctor said, in what you'd never have taken for an old man's voice. "You struggle, and you might find yourself with something important cut off. So make up your mind and grit your teeth. No moving now, whatever you do!"

I mean, hell—there was no anesthetic or anything in those days! He took a great slash at me with the knife right next to the balls, then twisted it sideways. I was prepared for the worst, but even so I felt faint, everything went black in front of my eyes, and I couldn't help letting out a shout.

Not that the doctor could have cared. In no time he'd carved out the buboes on both sides of my groin, then he stuck a thing like a metal spoon in the holes he'd made and dug around inside. I expect he was getting out the pus and rotten flesh. That was even worse than being cut with the knife; I just can't tell you what it was like.

The doctor gave me some medicine, and I went off with it, with Kyuzo holding me up. I was much too far gone to walk, so we got a rickshaw and I somehow made it home. I was more dead than alive, but you needn't think I just curled up and went to sleep. No—it was only after that that I came near to losing my life.

The Kawagoe doctor had told me to take some pills as soon as I got home. So I took them—but they must have been arsenic: it was hardly ten minutes before my whole body felt like it was on fire. My belly hurt as though it had molten lead in it. I just couldn't stand it.

I was groaning so loud that the maid heard me and gave a yell, which brought the chief clerk running. Before long I felt

33

as sick as a dog, and threw up. It was all blood. I got the runs too; that was all thick and bloody too, and it wouldn't stop. The next thing I knew, I was being bundled into a rickshaw and taken by my uncle to a hospital in Kanda. The doctor there took one look at me and said I hadn't got one chance in ten of pulling through. He gave me a hell of a lot of injections. I gradually lost consciousness, and when I came to it was daytime.

There wasn't anybody by my bed. I was lying by myself in a whitewashed room. The funny thing is, I didn't have any pain at all. The bleeding had stopped too, and by the evening of that day I was able to slurp up a bit of broth. I suppose my luck was still holding and, besides, I was a lot younger and tougher in those days.

Kyuzo came to see me as it was getting dark. "You gave everybody a scare," he said. "We thought you were a goner. But I'm glad you made it."

I left the hospital on the tenth day. "You're a tough fellow, I must say," the doctor told me as I was leaving. "But be careful with the women from now on. It might do you in the next time around."

Perhaps the Kawagoe doctor's kill-or-cure treatment worked; anyway, the syphilis never recurred, luckily enough. Oyone went off somewhere by herself. I only hope the same trouble didn't get her too. I'd never forgive myself if it did.

Midnight Boats

You know, there was an area they used to call "skid row."

As he spoke, the man poured some hot water from a thermos into the little teapot. His hand shook, and some of the water spilled onto the quilt over the sunken hearth where we were sitting. "Here, have some tea," he said. He handed me a cup and had a sip from his own before folding his arms and continuing his tale.

I'd got over my illness and gone back to my old work at last, but I'd not been back a month when something happened. It was early spring in the year of the Great Earthquake, so it must have been 1923.

I was going around with the coke every day as usual, but one day "Balloon" Shinkichi and "Soldier" Tarokichi, who normally went with me on deliveries, suddenly stopped turning up. I asked the foreman, but he didn't know what had happened to them, nor did the others. Then, about ten days later, Tarokichi showed up again. His eyes were staring and his face looked as if he hadn't had anything to eat for several days.

"What happened?" I asked. "Where's Shinkichi?"

"He's sick," he said. Then, without any more explanation, "Can you lend me ten yen?"

"Where d'you think I'd get ten yen from?" I said.

"No—" he said, "I mean, I want to borrow it from your uncle, I'll pay it back all right."

"But where's Shinkichi?" I asked again.

"Him?" he said. "He's had it."

"You serious?" I said.

"I know what a man's face looks like when he's going to die."

I could tell he wasn't kidding. So on condition that he took me to where Shinkichi was staying, an "inn" called the Meigetsukan, I told him I'd lend him some of the money my grandmother had given me when I left home.

The place they called "skid row" wasn't all that far from my uncle's firm, in Fukagawa. The whole area was crammed with flophouses; at the most there was only about a yard's space between them, so you had to turn sideways to get through the alleys. There's no telling how many of these "inns" there were altogether. The boards over the open drains had come off, and the sewage spilled over into the road; you got the stuff on you, all sticky and squelchy, as you walked.

There was only one time every day that really mattered in the area. Early in the morning, so early you could only just make people out in the dark, a scout would come and stand out in the middle of the road and yell "Hey, there!" and a couple of dozen men would come trickling out.

"There's unloading work at such-and-such a place," he'd shout. "Anybody who wants to go, put up your hand." And the hands would go up. The scout would pick some of them out by name. "The rest of you'll have to wait till next time," he'd say, and those left would move off without a word.

He'd check the number of men who were going to work that day and give them ten sen each. "Off you go, and be quick about it," he'd say in his bossy way. "I won't stand for any lateness."

And the men would dash off with their ten sen in their hands. You know where they were going? To the grub shop.

The people who lived in those parts never had any more money than they needed to keep them going that day. So most of the men hadn't had any breakfast. The first thing the scout did was give the guys he'd picked some money to have breakfast with; otherwise they'd be too hungry to work properly. As for the ones who didn't get any work—there was nothing they *could* do, so they just stayed put till something turned up.

The flophouses turned them out in the morning, so they had to stay out in the road. Whenever a scout came, they'd gather around him. If nothing came of it, they'd go on staying put. If there was nothing that day, they'd hope the next day would be better. And if it wasn't, then they stayed put till the next day again. Anyone who still had a bit of cash could go into a flophouse at night, but the rest were turned away. What did the guys do who didn't get work even on the third day? Nothing—just put up with not eating. Just stood around with their arms folded, drinking some water occasionally, making the best of it.

In that world, there were a few things you just never said. One was "I'm hungry"; the others were "I'm cold" and "I'm hot." As far as being hungry was concerned, they were all in the same boat, so it was a kind of competition to see who could bear it longest. If any of the men standing around there complained of being hungry, he'd be treated as an outsider, a slob who didn't have the guts to stick it out. They were all barely keeping going as it was, and for somebody to talk about food would have been the last straw.

It was the same with anyone who said he was cold. A loincloth more like a bit of rag, a single cotton kimono, and a small towel—that was all the property a man had. Even in winter with an icy wind blowing, they'd stand there in their loincloths and kimonos, putting up with it, trying to look as though they weren't cold, even though their bellies were empty and a wind was blowing fit to knock you over. It was the only shred of pride they had left.

After three days of steady rain with no work to be found and nothing to do, a man gets desperate. If your belly's rumbling and your head almost reeling, you feel like eating anything you find lying around, whatever it is. But they wouldn't let themselves become scavengers—they absolutely refused to pick up anything lying in the road, or take scraps from the grub shop. Anybody who gave in and did that would be sneered at for letting himself become a beggar. "I'd rather die than eat other people's garbage," they'd say. And if some guy who was doing OK said, "Here—I can't eat all this, you have it," they'd still refuse it, even if they hadn't eaten for days on end. "What d'you take me for? *I* don't want any leftovers!" That's the kind of place it was.

Don't get the idea that all the people living there were men: there were women, too. Whores, every one of them —women who used to work in the brothels in Yoshiwara, or Suzaki, or Monzen Nakacho, then got old or caught the clap and lost their jobs and drifted down the scale till they landed up there. They'd latch onto some man who'd found work and was a bit flush, and sell themselves on a straw mat spread out behind the lumber down by the river. They couldn't take time off just because they were a bit sick, or they'd got a temperature, or some skin trouble. Nobody helped them. So they went on selling their bodies till they rotted on them.

There were cheap eating places in between the flophouses, and shops selling booze. I saw a general store too, with straw sandals and other stuff hanging up front. The road was all pitted, with no proper ditches, so there was raw sewage around everywhere as we walked along on our way to the Meige-tsukan.

Suddenly, we saw a man lying in the middle of the road. His hair was graying, and he was muddy all over. A policeman was standing there shouting at him, with people peering out through partly opened doors and out of alleyways, wondering what was going on. There was a whore with a cotton towel on her head and a face all shrunk and wrinkled, looking in their direction.

The policeman was shouting, "Come on, you! You can't sleep in the gutter! Get up, you bastard!" But the gray-haired man stayed lying where he was. It was icy cold out there.

"Get up! D'you hear me, damn you?"

The policeman began to kick the man in the side with his boot.

"You can't stay here! It's no good pretending you're sick!"

The man staggered to his feet somehow, but he soon fell forward on his face again.

"Get up! Come on!" yelled the policeman, giving him another sharp kick.

"Let's go," Tarokichi said to me.

"What's he done?" I asked the cop.

"And who might *you* be?"

"Can't you see he'll die if he's left like this?"

"D'you think I don't know that?"

"Then why d'you have to kick him like that?"

Yes, I really said it, you know—it makes me smile to think of it now; I must have been pretty cocky for my age. Anyway, before I knew it the copper had let fly at me with his fist. When I came to, I was lying by the side of the road.

"You must be nuts," somebody said.

A woman laughed, showing her rotten teeth. Tarokichi was nowhere to be seen.

"What are you doing here?" another said.

"I'm looking for somebody.... What happened to the man who was here?" I asked.

"The old man? I rescued him," someone standing behind the woman said. "The cop told me to move him away, so I got him on my back and lugged him over to the other side of the road. Me, half starving as I am."

"So what happened then?"

"Well, what d'you think? The copper shoved off, so I took him and left him out there in the road again." And he laughed without making any sound, opening his mouth and showing his bad teeth. The thing was—according to what he said—it was a nuisance for the police if someone died in their own district. It meant they had to write reports, take care of the body, etc. So if there was any trouble on their beat, they moved it next door. If the person died there, it was the other district's responsibility. Of course, the same thing might happen in reverse, so they had to keep their eyes open. A man who was on his last legs would be kicked from one side of the street to the other, till in the end he dropped dead on the side that happened to be unlucky.

After a while I moved on, and by asking the way as I went, I managed to find the flophouse called the Meigetsukan. It was a makeshift building with a swarthy old man with a squashed-up face sitting at the entrance.

"Is Shinkichi here?" I asked.

"What business is it of yours?"

"I'm a friend."

"Got any money?"

"Has a man called Tarokichi been?"

"He cleared out, the bastard. So you'll have to pay the fellow's lodgings, at least."

40

I gave him some money, and he took me to where Shinkichi was lying. But, you know, Shinkichi was dead: I touched his forehead and it was like ice.

"He was alive till this morning," the old man said. "What a fine thing to happen!... It'll cost a bit more, if you've got any on you...."

So I gave him another yen, and he went straight off and came back with two scruffy-looking men.

The men talked to each other as they moved about the room.

"He hadn't been eating properly."

"This cotton coat isn't bad at all."

"I'm having the loincloth," said one of them, laughing, a pale flabby fellow with runny eyes. They stripped Shinkichi and put the body in a black bag. The smaller man put Shinkichi's kimono over his shoulders, on top of his own rags.

"Let's go, then."

"Sure we haven't left anything lying around?"

They cackled at each other, baring their yellow teeth, as they shouldered the bag and went out. I don't know what they did with Shinkichi. Tarokichi never showed up again from that day on.

Not long after Shinkichi died, I was summoned to my uncle's other house in Koishikawa. The whole district was full of printers' signs. My uncle's family spent the weekends there.

My uncle was waiting for me in his study.

"I'm thinking of bringing you here next month to have you do a bit of studying. A friend of mine runs an accountant's office, so you can go to learn the business. You can work as a houseboy here in the mornings and go there in the afternoons. Once you've learned accounting, I want you to work in my own office."

I agreed with this and left. I expect it was some word from my father back home that made my uncle come up with such a sudden suggestion. Personally, I didn't much fancy the idea of sitting at a desk all day with a pen in my hand. All the same, I wouldn't be able to stay in Tokyo if I disobeyed my uncle, and I didn't have anywhere to go if I ran away, either, so on my way back to the depot I was wondering what to do. Just about then, though, something cropped up—I suppose you could say my stars were unlucky at the time.

All kinds of people, and not just laborers, came to join in the gambling in the coal yard. One of them was a rather queer fellow. His name was Kenkichi, and he must have been about ten years older than me. He was a dark, skinny guy with bulging eyes and a mean kind of look. He hardly said a word all the time he was playing. He seemed to have plenty of money, and parted with it a good deal more freely than the laborers did.

I asked Kyuzo what he did for a living, but the only answer I got was "A boatman, I expect"; it seems Kyuzo didn't know much more than I did. I couldn't help wondering where Kenkichi got all that cash.

After a while he stopped coming, but then, on the day after I visited my uncle's other house, he suddenly turned up again. Kyuzo asked him what had happened, and he said he'd had a nasty bit of trouble thanks to a woman. She'd given him syphilis, and he got the usual swellings. He'd had them cut out but there'd been complications and he'd had to stay in bed for quite a while.

"Well, then, this lad beat you to it." Kyuzo told him what had happened to me, and we all had a good laugh. And from then on he somehow seemed to approve of me.

It was one day around the beginning of June when Ken-kichi asked me to go out with him that evening.

"Got anything interesting in mind?" I said.

"I'll tell you later," he said. "Anyway, be in front of the Tomioka Fudo shrine at eight o'clock this evening." There was something shifty about the way he said it, it made me curious, and I went to the place at the time we'd fixed. When I got there, there was a man standing half-hidden behind a ginkgo tree like he didn't want to be seen, a wrinkled-looking guy in a workman's half-coat.

"You're Eiji, right?" the man said, treading softly as he came up. He told me to follow him, and we started walking. He went incredibly fast. He had a cotton towel around his neck, but that was the only light-colored thing about him: everything else was black or gray; I'd have lost sight of him if I hadn't kept close. Before long, we came to a canal with a lighter alongside.

The man with me jumped down into the boat.

"So he came, did he?" a voice said. I peered into the darkness and thought I could make out Kenkichi.

"Come on board."

"It's pitch-dark, this boat," I said.

"We couldn't do business if it was light."

Kenkichi sat me down among the cargo. It was too dark to see anything.

"What do you think—how about helping me out with my work?"

"What kind of work is it?"

"Work that makes money."

"You don't mean stealing?"

"Stealing isn't my line."

"Then what *do* you do?"

"I'll tell you because I think I can trust you. This is a midnight boat."

A midnight boat

I'd heard about these boats from the laborers, but it was hard to believe this was really one of them. Their main job was to ferry goods and people around so they didn't get seen by the police. Nowadays, I guess, they use trucks, but it was all boats back then. According to Kenkichi, though, he ran a "clean" ship—no thieves in his business, apparently.

"What do you do if you get caught?" I asked.

"You worry about that when it happens. It's safe enough so long as you stick to the routine."

"Sounds interesting," I said.

"It takes guts. But it's profitable," he said.

That was how I came to work on a midnight boat, based in

Fukagawa. We had various clients, some of them prosperous-looking men who you could see at a glance had their own businesses. Some people mightn't believe any respectable person would have traveled on a boat like that, but you can't be expected to understand unless you know how the police used to work.

In the old days, they were really something to be scared of. If they thought there was anything at all suspicious about you, you were hauled straight off to a police box and given the once-over. So anybody who had anything on his conscience was always extra careful not to catch their eye.

There were any number of rivers and canals in Fukagawa, and a lot of bridges to go with them. At one end of the main bridges, there was almost always a police box where they kept a watch on people who went by. In the daytime, of course, there were too many people passing by for them to question everybody, but if you were walking along late at night you were bound to get stopped.

The way most Japanese lived before the war, you got up while it was still dark and went to work, went hard at it all day, then came home when it got dark, had a meal, and went to bed, which meant that in most families everybody was asleep by around nine. So if anyone was out on the streets at that time of night, they assumed he couldn't be up to any good.

"Hey, you there! Yes, you—come over here. What have you been up to to make you this late?"

"Work."

"Work? What d'you mean, work? Why should you be working as late as this?"

Once the cops had got their hands on you, they didn't let go of you in a hurry. "Where do you work?" "Who's your boss?" All kinds of things they asked, and if you couldn't

45

answer promptly they'd knock you around a bit and as often as not take you into custody till the morning. If it happened that you'd been gambling and had a fair bit of money in your pocket and got nabbed on the way home, you'd had it. You were arrested on the spot and sent straight to the lockup. So the regular players were always worried about how they were going to get home, and the guys running the games were always trying to find ways of getting them past the trouble spots.

Fukagawa was more of a problem in that way than most places, because you couldn't get home without crossing those bridges. So they got up to all kinds of tricks; one of them was tying a player's purse up with string and throwing it across to him. The way it was done was this: you'd tie the thing up with a long piece of string, the kind you use on kites, and fix a stone to the other end. The guy then gave you the purse a good way this side of the bridge, and went on empty-handed. And, sure enough, the policeman there would stop him for questioning.

"Where are you going at this time of night?"

"Well, you see, a friend of mine wasn't well, so I've been to see him."

"I've heard that one before."

"It's true, I promise you."

"Then I'll go and check up with him tomorrow. Put out all your belongings on the table here."

"Yes, sir."

The man would lay out everything he had on him for inspection. If asked to, he'd have to let them look inside his bellyband and even his loincloth, too.

"Is that all?"

"Absolutely."

"Right—and from now on, mind you're not out this late again."

And with that bit of advice, they'd let him go. After crossing, he'd make a detour till he got to the bank opposite where you were waiting, then toss a stone in your direction. When you got the signal, you'd throw the stone tied to the string over to the other side. The guy would pick it up and give it a tug or two. That told you it was all right, and you'd let go.

Actually, though, it wasn't all that good a method. For one thing, the purse obviously got wet, and if it was too far across the river, you couldn't reach the other side. Also, if you went past a police box too many times in the same month, they naturally got suspicious, whether you were carrying a purse or not. So people usually took a roundabout route home, using deserted alleys. Another way, with customers who had plenty of time, was to let them play on till morning, then ask them to leave as soon as it got light. But for people who absolutely had to get home in a hurry while it was still dark, there was a special method. That was the midnight boat.

Most of these were set up for thieves, wanted criminals, smuggled goods, and anything else that needed hiding from the police; but Kenkichi specialized in gamblers.

Somebody would call, "Passenger for you!" The boat would come alongside with a thump, and someone would jump on board. There'd be another call from up on the bank: "He's yours, then, skipper," and a "Right!" from down here.

The passenger was then led in among the piles of cargo, and a big black cloth was pulled down so that it covered him completely.

"Stand by," Kenkichi would say, and the boat would glide

away from the bank. The river would show up in little black, silver, or copper-colored waves. The houses would all be in darkness. There was a regulation saying that boats using the river at night should always carry lights, but this one didn't. It slid along secretly, without a sound, in the pitch dark. Nobody spoke. The only thing you could hear was the sound of the water. For someone not used to it, the thrill was enough to make your balls shrink.

At that time all the main waterways had lookout posts on them. They'd been there for centuries, and they kept a round-the-clock watch on anything afloat. Wherever two canals crossed or met in a T shape, there'd be a lookout, so there was no question of going via those places. It was the same with any bridge that had a police box: if anybody happened to look over the railing, you were obviously in trouble. Even without police boxes, though, there was always a chance of being caught by a cop on patrol. So we moved in the shadows close to the bank, slow enough to be able to stop at short notice; and we kept our own lookout men on shore, walking along on each side of us, a little way in front.

As soon as one of them saw a copper coming, he'd chuck a stone as a signal, and get himself hidden away behind something. Kenkichi would quickly pull in to the side and stay put. You see, there were so many other boats around that once we'd stopped we were usually safe. If helped, too, that we could count on the other boatmen to turn a blind eye. If they'd given us away, they risked—well, policemen poking around on their own boat, for one thing—but also being out-lawed by the other people working on the river, and being driven out of business.

Then, when the coast was clear, we'd slip quietly away, and move on down the dark river.

The Bricklayer

There were no bunks on our boat, so Kenkichi arranged for me to stay at the home of a man called Tokuzo, who was in charge of a crew of raftsmen. By now the timberyards have shifted out into Tokyo bay and there's no trace of the old Fukagawa left, but when I was there Fukagawa meant only one thing: timber. There were timberyards and timber wholesalers everywhere you went—hundreds of wholesalers alone.

Timber rafts in Fukagawa

Timber was floated down to Fukagawa from all over Japan; by the old way of reckoning it would have been worth millions of *koku* of rice. The logs were then left to float in the timberyards, where merchants bought and sold them. Whenever they towed the stuff they'd bought to the lumbermill, or when they wanted it brought ashore, the raftsmen would take care of everything that had to be done. Their foremen kept

49

"stables," where they trained the men.

Each foreman usually had about thirty people working for him, so they had to have big rooms for everybody to eat and sleep in. Those rooms were just the place for gambling. The raftsmen didn't do much of it among themselves, though, and players came in from outside.

Serious gambling isn't all that popular nowadays, but in my time all kinds of people—the owners of large shops or classy restaurants, for instance—used to go in for it in a big way. Gambling was a big thing at Tokuzo's place too; there was hardly a day when there wasn't a session.

Maybe I'd better say a bit at least about the dice games at our stable. A professional was in overall charge, and the foreman just supplied a room, he wasn't personally involved. You sometimes get scenes in movies showing "the good old days" of gambling, but they always mess it up. For one thing, a gambling joint was a *quiet* place; nobody ever shouted. After all, they weren't supposed to be doing what they were doing, and they were afraid of being caught, so they kept quiet in case people passing outside got wind of it.

The actual game was run by a man called a *nakabon*, a bookie.

"Evens, odds ... right, place your bets," the bookie would say in a soft, deep voice.

"Odds still to go." All the rest were quiet, so his voice sounded quite intense, and there'd be a kind of keyed-up atmosphere.

"No more odds. No more odds. Evens still to go. Evens, evens."

This meant the odds were all covered, with no further bets being taken there. Until someone bet on even, though, the game couldn't move along.

"Anyone for evens? No dice till there's a bet."

People follow their own hunches on how the dice will roll; but when the game's held up with "evens still to go" everybody gets impatient, so at least one person usually gives in, just to keep things going. When enough chips are out, the bookie then calls, "Right—stop. Odds and evens are covered. Here goes!" And the "shooter" turns the dice cup upside down on the red cloth spread out between the rows of players. That moment when he slams the cup down—that's the best part of the whole thing, you know.

Workers like the raftsmen didn't have much cash, so they weren't all that popular. The people who were really welcome—it's obvious why—were elderly landowners, rich men's wives, and so on.

Everybody wanted to win of course, but people came as much for the atmosphere as for the gambling. So the important thing was to see that even if they lost they went home feeling OK. In movies and plays you sometimes see a guy getting thrown out of a game after losing his shirt to some professional; but that's a load of rubbish. I mean, if you did that kind of thing and the customer happened to tell the police, everyone who'd had anything to do with the game would be pulled in.

Besides, anybody who lost so much at gambling that it ruined him once and for all wouldn't be able to come again, and word would get around that it was that kind of place. And that would be the end of it. So if someone started losing too heavily, the boss would have a word with him—something soothing, like "Look, sir, you don't seem to be in luck this evening. Why don't you call it a day?" And he'd give him a bit of money and say, "Here's something to get home with—it's on the house."

The professional gambler was quite different from gangsters nowadays. He was more like a master craftsman, who happened to make his living by the dice. It paid to be considerate—no one who was just out to make a profit at other people's expense would have kept going for long in that business.

One of the players who always appealed to me was the madam of a brothel in Monzen Nakacho. She was filthy rich, but her man apparently gave her a bad time; she was always in a stew about something, and she'd gamble to get it off her chest. She was always in a hurry, too; she'd come in and without even taking her cape off she'd fish a great purse out of her sash and say, "Now what am I supposed to do? Which side is still short? Evens? Not enough evens? Right—evens it is!" and she'd plonk down a pile of money. She won sometimes, but with that way of doing things you always lose in the long run, so her purse would soon be a lot lighter. Even so, she seemed to feel better for it.

"Now I *enjoyed* that," she'd say to the boss. "Thanks." And off she'd rush again.

She was in such a tearing hurry that you never felt you could settle down to the game properly if she was there, but she was one of the better customers just the same.

Another one was a man we called "Sei-chan the bricklayer." We took him on the midnight boat any number of times, but I'm not likely to forget the first time he showed up at the gambling joint. He had brand-new leather-soled sandals and wore a fancy silk kimono tied with a shiny sash and a gold chain that must have been a good half inch thick dangling on his chest, with this huge gold watch to match at the end. He was lavish with his money too, he'd chuck it down as if it was so much wastepaper; if he lost, he'd just laugh it off. He was a bit below average in height, and plump, with bulging eyes; you'd never have called him a good-looking man, but even so he had this air of authority, as if to say: I'm the boss where I come from. He made such an impression on me that I asked Tameji what he did. Tameji was only a couple of years older than me, but he already passed as a first-rate raftsman.

"Him? That's Sei-chan the bricklayer."

"That's a funny name."

"Seems his father was a master bricklayer, but the son was light-fingered even when he was young. His dad threw him out, and now he's master of another trade." And Tameji bent his right index finger into a hook shape, meaning a pickpocket.

"Is he? You'd never think it to look at him, would you?"

"I know, but he's got real clout. He's got dozens of people working for him. The whole Asakusa area is his territory."

No wonder he could afford to throw his money around like that! I was kind of impressed, you know, and I used to watch what he did. Sometimes, as I said, Sei-chan came on our boat, and one night just as he was stepping off onto the bank he said to me,

"Hey, Eiji—how about coming to do the sights of Asakusa tomorrow? I'll be at the Niomon gate at twelve o'clock. All right? I'll be expecting you."

The idea caught my fancy, so I thought I might as well stroll over and take a look. Those two fierce-looking statues in the gate—they're a fine pair. I was waiting in front of them when Sei-chan came along with one of his men. He was wearing a kimono of handmade Oshima silk, with that great long gold chain dangling in a showy way in front. He was so got up, you'd have taken him for some rich hick up from the country.

53

We strolled along till we came to the main building of the temple, where they keep the statue of Kannon.

"Look at that!" he said proudly. "The greatest of all the Kannons in Japan! Asakusa owes everything it's got to this Kannon.

"Here—" he said, holding out something, "my offering." I looked, and it was a one-yen bill. Then he smiled and flashed his gold teeth at me and said, "You'll never get lucky if you're mean with your offerings." And he got another one-yen bill out of his wallet and threw it into the offertory box, then pressed his pudgy hands together in front of him and bowed his head to the Buddha. After that we wandered past the souvenir shops leading up to the temple, then went into a sukiyaki restaurant called Imahan.

The manager and a maid were in the entrance hall to welcome us.

"The boss says he'll treat you to anything you feel like," said his bodyguard.

I was reasonably well off myself around that time, but I didn't like to offend him, so I decided to say nothing and let him treat me. That was the first time in my life I ever had sukiyaki. You know, even now, I always remember Sei-chan whenever I eat the stuff.

Sei-chan seemed to be concerned about me.

"Tell me," he said, "just how long do you aim to stay on that boat? I can tell you, it's all hard work, and it won't last long.

"They say you're related to the coal merchant in Ishijima-cho. Your father's not going to be very pleased to hear you're on a midnighter.... How much do they pay you?"

"I'm not hard up."

"I don't suppose you are, but I'm sure it doesn't come anywhere near what we make. Look, there's something I'd like to ask you. Why don't you join my staff? I'll see you're well looked after. You'd get to know the job a bit at a time. You could have your keep for a while without doing anything in particular. It'd be much more fun for you in Asakusa than wasting your time hanging around a timberyard."

It seems Sei-chan had decided I was suitable recruiting material. Quite an honor! To me, I already felt like a grown man, but in his eyes I guess I was still just a kid: someone who had the makings of a good pickpocket, given the right education....

Sei-chan was drinking as we ate, and after a while he got quite cheerful. I hadn't agreed to join his crowd, of course, but he seemed to feel he could talk me into it, given time. I was in quite a fix.

Just then his bodyguard suddenly said, "I think he's coming."

I saw a man hurrying toward us, a short man with a nasty look in his eyes and the kind of face that had pickpocket written all over it.

"Boss—we finally caught him," the man said, looking very pleased with himself.

"Where?"

"On the train."

"Didn't he put up a fight?"

"There were three of us, and Tiny was one of them. You can't do much against a former Sumo wrestler." He gave a nasty little giggle, then opened his rattrap of a mouth to ask, "What shall we do about it?"

"You don't need me to tell you, do you?"

"D'you want us to ...?"

"Yes," Sei-chan answered, as if it didn't matter much.

In the yakuza world, they sometimes cut off a little finger, but among pickpockets a person who's poached on someone else's territory loses the forefinger of his working hand.

The guy gave me a sort of sidelong look and trotted out again. None of this seemed to spoil the other two's mood. Sei-chan went on buttering me up, then gave me ten yen: "Here—" he said, "here's some pocket money."

People are liable to get annoyed if you refuse something they've offered you, so I took it and was grateful. But then he reached inside his kimono and said, "I can give you more if it's not enough."

That shook his sidekick: "You'll get him into bad habits if you give him that much," he said, and it occurred to me, too, that it'd be risky to accept any more.

Sei-chan had some meeting or other later that afternoon, he said. He paid the bill, then before he went off he said to me, "Any time you like. Just come to the address on this card and I'll be ready to discuss things with you, any time. Think it over, anyway."

The name card was a grand affair with a gold border, and on it it said:

Takamuro Seizaburo
Specialist
in
Trouble of All Kinds

Riots

It was around the end of spring in the year of the Great Earthquake. The weather was perfect, and I was lying dozing on the boat when I woke up and saw Kenkichi close by me. He was sitting there quietly with a frown on his forehead as though he was thinking about something, so I didn't say anything. But then he suddenly looked at me with a serious expression and said—it took me by surprise—"It's no wonder Sei-chan's worried about you. You're not going to do yourself any good by staying on this boat."

"Well, then," I asked him, "how come you got into the business yourself?"

He grinned. "I come from a different background to you," he said. Then almost at once he went back to looking gloomy, and sat for a long time without saying anything. Normally, he had that kind of shadow over him that you see with people in that kind of life, but this time it was somehow different. He was leaning on the edge of the boat looking up at the sky. I can see him now, his hair with its white streaks fluffed up in the evening breeze, as he started telling me his story.

"I don't expect you've heard of them, but in 1907 there were big riots at the Ashio copper mines. I was in Ashio myself at the time, working in the mines. I got mixed up in the disturbances and ran away from the job. What really started it all for me in the first place was that I was an orphan.

"My mother was a stupid woman. She was the daughter of a wealthy farmer, but she had an illegitimate kid—that was me—then went and died when I was eleven. She was only twenty-nine herself. I heard that my father was a traveling

57

salesman who called at the house regularly, but I never met him.

"They held the funeral with as little fuss as possible, and as soon as it was over I ran away from home. There was an uncle of my mother's who ran a sawmill back in the hills of Numata in Gumma prefecture; I'd been to stay with him just once with my mother, when I was seven. He was a nice man, I won't forget him. He did all kinds of things to try and cheer my mother up. I remember her kneeling in front of him with her head bowed right down to the floor, crying.

"The children living round about used to come and play with me, but they didn't tease me, which was a surprise. We used to play together in the river that ran down the valley; for me, it was all like a dream, with the sound of the woodsmen working in the hills, and the birds chirping away. I'd never known there were places like that. Maybe my mother was hoping to leave me there. Either way, she was disappointed, and we went back home in tears.

"After my mother died, I decided it'd be best to go and try my luck there. I walked for days on end, but when I finally got there I found my uncle had died and the sawmill had passed into somebody else's hands. I didn't have anywhere else to go, so I worked there for a while helping a packhorse man. The work meant taking the trees the foresters had felled down to the sawmill, but I was too small to be much use. I used to put the ropes around the timber and untie them again later, clean up around the mill, wash the horses, and other things like that, getting bawled out all the time.

"I gradually got to be able to handle the horses on my own, and started taking the lumber from the mill to the yards. I used to load on a little more wood than I was supposed to be carrying, and take it to a general store where I knew the people. They'd buy it from me, and I'd use the money to buy myself some buns and save a bit on the side. I mean, the pack-horse man would never have given me a single bun even if he'd had ten himself. He didn't give me a penny in wages, either. So I'd have starved in time if I hadn't learned to look after myself.

"Then, in the year that I turned sixteen, a man who came to recruit laborers for the Ashio copper mines asked me if I'd care to work there. They paid one yen a day, he said. I jumped at the chance. Five others were taken on besides me, and we set off on foot.

"The whole way it was nothing but hills and mountains. We went so far up into the hills you'd never have thought any-body could live there. But after we'd been walking I don't know how many days, the man from the mine suddenly pointed and said,

" 'That's Ashio, over there.'

"I couldn't believe my eyes. 'God, just look at those hills!' I said, goggling.

"Everywhere you looked, the hills were bare. Not a tree in sight, not a blade of grass. We kept on up a narrow valley, and then got an even bigger shock: you see, there was a town, a proper town, there.

"There was a town hall and a hospital. An iron bridge over the river to take the trollies from the mines. Electric locomo-tives to haul trains carrying the ore. There was a hydroelectric power station, and the town had electric lighting. None of us had ever seen electric light before, and we were bowled over.

"It was a fantastically busy place. Every kind of shop you could think of. There were lots of inns, too—one of them was where all the people connected with the copper mines stayed, and it had a telephone. There was a photo studio as well, which had some connection with the mines, but they'd photograph you any time so long as you paid for it. That was something new to us, so we had our pictures taken to celebrate. There were two or three geisha houses, and four brothels. Two theaters, too, which opened whenever a traveling troupe came. I'd say the population was something over thirty thousand. It was a really lively place, what with miners, merchants, government officials, and women and children all stuck together in that little bit of space between the hills. We were as pleased as punch—told ourselves we'd come to a wonderful place. But things aren't like that in real life.

"I won't go on about it too much, because you can't imagine what it was like unless you'd actually been there, but the toughest thing about our work was the blasting, using dynamite. Every time they set off a charge, it was like being inside the barrel of a cannon instead of a mine shaft. The dust swirled right through the shaft, blocking your nose so you couldn't breathe.

"To start with, I was put to work with an iron thing like a rake, using it to clear up bits of ore that had broken off, and waste rock; but I was scared all the time in case they were going to set off the dynamite. I kept this up for about two years, but then, around the beginning of February 1907, something happened that I'll never forget.

"A great chunk of the tunnel roof caved in, and I was one of the unlucky ones who got caught. Everything went black, you couldn't see a thing. I was half buried, with my arms and legs trapped and steadily going numb. I told myself this was the end. Then there was another fall, a great rush of smaller bits of rock. I got a lot of dust or something in my mouth and up my nose, choking me. It was sheer torture.

"This is it, I thought, I can't put up with this. But something in me refused to give up. It got steadily worse. Hell, I thought, if dying is as bad as this, I'm damned if I'm going to die! I lay there struggling with my left arm, which I could move just a bit, then somehow I managed to cough out the muck in my mouth, so at least I could breathe. I yelled for help at the top of my voice. When I did, I heard voices coming from both directions. A dim light came close up to me and someone said,

" 'You all right?'

" 'The fuck I am!' I said.

" 'If you can talk like that *you're* not going to die,' the voice said. 'There are some poor devils still buried. You wait where you are for a while.' And they went off to look for the other men.

"I stayed put—not that I could do anything else—but I was sure that if there was another fall I'd be a goner. I got really mad at them, wondering how long it'd be before they got me out.

"They finally rescued me a few hours later—but we were still in the tunnel; the fall had blocked the way out, and it was impossible to get up to the surface. There'd been a lot of men working with us, and a hell of a lot of them, it seems, had been killed. Less than thirty had survived altogether.

"One of the survivors was Kihachi, the sub-foreman, and he took charge of everything. It was he that decided who was going to use the batteries we had left, who was going to look for escape routes, and what the daily ration of water would be. Everyone held on grimly, doing just as Kihachi said.

"It was two days later that they got us out. We'd all been telling ourselves we'd never breathe the outside air again, so I can't tell you what it was like when we finally knew we were safe.

"The other men, up above, were pleased to see us looking livelier than they'd expected. We were telling them about how the cave-in happened and what it was like in the tunnel, when someone began talking about the miners who'd been killed. That gradually got everybody worked up, and they started cursing the officials in the mining office. Then, before long, they decided they ought to have a drink in memory of their dead mates.

" 'Let's go to the office,' someone said. 'We'll get the people there to come up with some saké.'

" 'That's right,' everybody shouted. 'We'll get the office bastards to provide it!'

" 'That's not enough—we ought to shave their heads for them!'

"By now they'd worked up a real head of steam, and more and more men were joining them. In the end, we all marched off toward the office, with the miners who'd been rescued in the lead. But we found a couple of dozen security guards standing in the road there, blocking the way.

" 'No entry! Break it up there!'

" 'Who d'you think *you* are to order us around? Get out of the way!'

" 'No, get back!'

"The same kind of shouting match went on, with us gradually shoving the security people back, till a line of police suddenly came bursting in.

"That only got everybody more excited, and it was just about to turn into a real fight when suddenly behind us there was this terrific explosion. I looked, and there were flames shooting up. Some of the miners had blown up the stables with dynamite. Kihachi set off running, with us following. He crept into the office from the back, where the guards weren't watching, and got up onto the fuel storage sheds.

" 'Break the roof in!' he yelled.

"We made a hole in the corrugated iron and jumped down inside—ten of us in all, I'd say. Kihachi handed each of us a bundle of dynamite, fuses, cans of kerosene and so on, then splashed kerosene over the floor and led a fuse from it outside.

" 'Go and smash things up,' he said to us, '—the other buildings, the town hall, anything you come across. Just let yourselves go!'

"He set light to the fuse, we cleared out, then a great flame shot up and there was an almighty explosion. After that it was like a hurricane had hit the place. We overturned trollies and blocked the road, cut power lines and telephone cables. We set fire to anything we could. Several hundred miners attacked the boss's official residence, smashing up everything that came in reach. The boss himself was beaten up, and anybody who was any kind of official at the mine got clobbered too. The rioting went on like that for three days. I was by Kihachi's side all the time, but toward the end he told me to get out, it was getting too risky.

" 'I'm not going to run away,' I said.

" 'Don't be dumb. The troops'll be here before long and you know what'll happen then, so get out while the going's good.'

" 'What about you?'

" 'I'm leaving too, of course. But I'm the one who started it all, so they'll hunt all over for me. *You're* OK—your name's not known. Take to the hills and keep going, straight south. If you do that and can get away to Tokyo, nobody's ever going to find you. When you get to Tokyo, go to the end of Namida bridge in Senju, there's a place there where the day laborers

63

hang out, and ask for a man called Shugoro. Tell him I sent you, and he'll take care of you. I'll be following you before long, so get going.'

"So I made a break for it, over the hills. I heard later that soon after that the troops went into Ashio to put down the riots. I went on running for all I was worth, not even bothering to eat or drink, till I got to the foothills of Mt. Akagi, where I felt just too tired and hungry to go on. I was wandering about in a kind of daze when I met an old woodcutter. He took one look at me and said,

" 'You on the run from Ashio?'

"I didn't see any point in keeping it from him, so I nodded.

" 'Follow me,' he said, and he took me to a charcoal burner's hut. There he gave me a riceball and some broth.

" 'Where are you going next?' the old man asked.

" 'Tokyo,' I told him.

" 'Well, then, you'd better put these on,' he said, and he gave me some farmer's clothes. 'If you wear these and carry a bundle of charcoal, nobody's going to suspect you.'

"I thanked him and moved on, heading for the plain below. I never knew what it was made him help me in that way.

"It was about two weeks later that I met Shugoro near the bridge in Senju. He knew all about the Ashio affair. He told me I'd better lie low a while, so I worked there for about six months.

"While I was there I met a boatman called Jimpei. When he heard who I was, he said it would be safer if he took me in himself. Shugoro, too, told me he thought that would be best, so he brought me here—to this boat. When I first started work on it, Jimpei was still the skipper, but he died and I took over from him.... I never saw anything more of Kihachi."

The Monkeys' Money

"How long did you stay on the boat?" I asked the man.

"Not all that long."

As he spoke, he began to heave himself up off the cushion he was sitting on.

"Excuse me a moment, will you?" he said. Supporting himself on the edge of the hearth, he slowly started to get up, but the bottom of his kimono got tangled with his legs and he had trouble getting upright. Taking hold of a stick that stood propped against a pillar, he opened the sliding doors and went out into the corridor. Beyond the outer glass doors, I could see the rain pouring down from the eaves. A clock struck nine. I heard the man talking to somebody in the back room. After a while, though, the boards in the corridor creaked and he reappeared.

"You can't get around so well when you get older, can you?" he said.

"Perhaps I'd better go soon," I suggested.

"Do you have some work to do?"

"No, but you seem to be tired."

"Nonsense," he said. "What would I be doing going to bed at this time of day?" He put his hands under the quilt over the sunken hearth and, sitting hunched up, coughed thickly again and again.

It was in September 1923 that I stopped working on the boat. As you know, the first of that month was the day of the Great Earthquake.

Kenkichi and me and a girl called Iyo, a worker in a spinning mill who was due to become Kenkichi's wife, were having a meal in a place in Monzen Nakacho. Just then, there was this awful rumbling sound and the room began to sway. The china bowls and dishes and other things up on the shelves came raining down. A two-story house on the other side of the road lurched over to one side, then all of a sudden collapsed.

We knew right off this wasn't any ordinary quake. We'd have been crushed under the building if we'd stayed put, so we scrambled out, started running, and kept going till we got to the canal. But a warehouse right by the boat we'd left tied up there had collapsed, and the boat was half sunk. It was useless, and poor Kenkichi really took it hard. "God, look at that!" he kept saying. "I'll never be able to use it again."

Before long the sky began to turn red.

"It's the mill!" yelled Iyo, and she began to run again; the Amagasaki spinning mill where she worked was pouring smoke. So we set off after her. The fires were spreading at a terrific rate.

Morishita-cho was already a sea of flames. People were in a real panic, with old folk and children yelling at the top of their lungs.

"It's no good," said Kenkichi, grabbing at Iyo to hold her back. "There's nothing you can do even if we get to the mill."

A policeman was bellowing in a hoarse voice, "Go to the Army Clothing Depot!"

We ignored him and went on running steadily in the opposite direction. When we got to Eitai bridge we found that the whole area on the other bank, for hundreds of yards from Nihombashi on to Asakusa, was like a roaring furnace. Looking back, we saw that the fires were right behind us, too. A whirlwind had got up, and we saw a cart being blown high up into the air. Bits of houses and roofs were being sucked up into the whirlwind too and were dancing about in the sky like

66

leaves. A horse that had gone crazy was galloping about the street and finally jumped into the river.

We decided we'd try to get to the Clothing Depot and went on blindly, forcing our way through the waves of people. It had got dark before we noticed, and the fires were getting fiercer and fiercer. Just as we reached a point slightly beyond the Oshima river, there was a great roar and a huge column of red flames went up. The Clothing Depot, which had also caught fire, had fallen in. It made your flesh crawl—the whole night sky rocking with screams and shrieks. There'd been thousands of people inside.

The Great Earthquake

I gave up any hope of getting through safely; whatever happened now, I thought, we'd had it. But it was too hot to stand around, so we let ourselves be carried on by the crowd, on in the direction of Aikawa bridge. It was packed solid on the bridge too, so tight you could hardly move. Then, of course, people's belongings started to catch fire. If we hadn't done something, we'd have been burned alive.

Just then, we noticed a barge below us, under the bridge.

"I'm going in!" Kenkichi shouted, and jumped in with Iyo in his arms. I went in straight after them. There were dozens of people already on the barge, and someone soon helped us on board. But in no time hundreds of people were jumping from the bridge, with lots of them grabbing hold of the boat and trying to clamber in. A handful of them made it, but the barge looked like sinking at any moment.

"Keep off! The boat's full!" somebody on board bellowed.

"Are you going to leave us to die?" someone in the water shouted back. But then a sudden wind got up, the barge was carried away like a chip of wood, and we drifted off in the direction of the Merchant Sailors' School. That was on fire too, a big building, all ablaze. We panicked again for a moment, but the wind switched direction without warning, and we slowly drifted away till we fetched up at Tsukuda island, where the Sumida runs into the bay. It was one of the few places in that old part of Tokyo near the bay that were still standing quite undamaged.

We got off the barge and looked back at the city. The flames were even more terrible by now, shooting right up into the sky. It hardly seemed possible that we could have got through all that, all three of us, without being separated.

When dawn came, everywhere on the other side was just a blackened waste. Hundreds of bodies had been washed up at the water's edge. The awful thing about human beings, though—the survivors, I mean—is that even at times like that their bellies need feeding just the same as usual. Our throats were dry and sore, too. Something would have to be done about it. Not that we could very well pester the people living on the island for food: far too many people had taken shelter there for that.

So we decided to split up and hunt for something. I'd been there lots of times to deliver coke, and I knew the area. I walked steadily along the shore toward the east. After a while, I came to a bit of reclaimed land that was covered with thick grass.

I searched in the grass, looking for something—insects, anything—to eat. And then I found them—locusts, whole swarms of them, just sitting there on the long stalks of grass. I went racing around, catching them. I didn't have anything to put them in, so I took off my kimono, tied up the sleeves, and used them as bags. Two hours at it, and they were full. I brought them back, and the three of us ate them, raw. That took the edge off the hunger at least.

The next day, there were other people in the grass, and the locusts had all been caught. Search as much as you liked, there wasn't a single one left. I cursed and swore, but it didn't do any good. Then Kenkichi suggested we go and see if any emergency food centers had been set up.

Iyo said she couldn't walk any more, so we left her lying inside a damaged boat. We crossed the bridge, which was badly burned, into Fukagawa. Everywhere you went there were piles of corpses; nothing but black ruins and bodies in every direction. I don't know how long we walked, but though we heard plenty of rumors of relief centers we never actually got to find one. We only got steadily tireder and tireder and hungrier and hungrier, till we were almost fit to drop.

It was somewhere around Koume-cho in Honjo, I suppose—Kenkichi suddenly said, "Look—monkeys!" He was right, there were three of them, lying all snug together under a tree. A big monkey and two small ones.

"Maybe they're having a nap," he said as we went up to them.

"It's a funny place to find monkeys, though," I said.

But they weren't monkeys, they were human beings. A mother and two children, burned to death. Their bodies had shrunk, you see, and made them look like that. The mother was holding the smaller kid tight in her arms.

"Whatever happens, a mother never stops loving her kids," Kenkichi said, and we both put our hands together and said a prayer for them. But just then we saw something shiny on the mother's chest.

"Hey—what's that?"

We lifted her up—she weighed next to nothing, like cinders—and a lot of silver coins clattered down from her. There were a hell of a lot of them—a good basinful, I'd say.

"We've struck it rich!"

"Watch it—there are people coming."

I looked around and saw a line of people in the distance with bundles on their backs.

"If the emergency patrols find us that'll be the end of it."

We picked up all the money in a hurry, but as we were doing this I got a glimpse of what looked like a wad of banknotes down between her breasts.

"Hey! There's a fortune here!" I yelled. "How the hell did it survive?"

She must have soaked the bills in water or something, then put them in a money belt, because only the outside ones were burned.

"Shit! I can't get at them," Kenkichi said. "The kid's in the way."

He'd got the bills between his fingers and was trying to pull them out, but they wouldn't come. The kid clinging to its

70

mother was stopping them.

Kenkichi got impatient. "Pull them apart," he said. I tried, but they were too firmly stuck together.

"If I do it too hard, its arm'll come off."

"What does that matter? They're dead."

So I pulled again, and suddenly the kid's scorched skin slipped off so you could see the pulpy red flesh underneath. I had something nasty sticking to the palm of my hand. I got the feeling the kid was sort of eyeing me—it gave me the creeps.

"Let's pack it in," I said. "It's looking at me as if it *knows*. No good'll come of it, taking a woman's money like this."

"Don't be dumb."

"I've had enough."

"Well, don't come whining to me for money later, then."

Kenkichi got the mother and the kid apart. A good deal of the skin came off its arm, but the arm itself stayed put, and one bit of it, all blackened and small, was still fastened to its mother's body.

"There!" said Kenkichi, "we managed it, didn't we?" He took off his underwear, stuffed it full of money, and tied it around his waist.

"With this much cash, you know, I can get a new boat made...," he said. "Let's get out of here."

"You'd better go on your own."

"What d'you mean?"

"I'm quitting. Don't worry, I won't tell anybody."

Kenkichi walked off without so much as glancing back, and the mother and her kids, now separated, went on lying there on the ground.

Just as an afterthought: I might seem to be making excuses for Kenkichi, but I don't think you can really blame him. Up until the time of the earthquake, the woman and her kids had probably had an easy life in the kind of family that could afford a crowd of servants. They wouldn't have ended up like that if it wasn't for the money. Without the money, I expect they'd have been left in peace after they died, without getting pulled apart.

An Apprentice

Tokuzo, the raftsmen's foreman, had got away to his other house, together with the people from his stable, and they were safe.

The man took an advertising flier from between the pages of that day's newspaper, and used a felt pen to draw a map of the burned areas on the back.

This is where the fires were. It was the only place in his neighborhood that wasn't burned down, so he was really lucky. By the time I'd split up with Kenkichi and went to have a look, the first house was gone without a trace, but they'd got a temporary shack up, and everybody was hard at work. You see, a good half of Tokyo had been destroyed, so it was obvious the timberyards were going to have more business than they could cope with. I don't care what it is, I said, but let me do something to help. Tokuzo was really grateful—said they were so overworked they'd thought of asking the cat to lend a hand.

So they decided I should do odd jobs in the kitchen and around the house until things got back to something like normal. That bought me into contact every day with the fishmonger, the greengrocer, the tofu man, and the other people who came around selling things, and I was soon on good terms with all of them. Looking back on it now, I'd say I never had it so easy as around that time. But it didn't last all that long, as the next spring, early in April, someone who changed the whole course of my life came to visit.

He was a gang boss called Momose Umetaro; his territory included the entire Yanagibashi district in those days, and it seemed he and our foreman were sworn "brothers." That's what they used to call two men from different organizations who'd promised to help each other whenever necessary. Anyway, he turned up in a rickshaw that day, bringing one of his men with him.

When I took some tea in to them, Momose glanced at me and said to Tokuzo, "Brother, who's this young fellow here? I haven't seen him around before, have I?"

Tokuzo told him who I was. It seemed to get him interested.

"I see...," he said. "Quite a guy, eh? Tell me, then, how does he fit in with things?"

While he was asking this sort of thing, I was out in the corridor again, sitting just out of sight behind the sliding doors, as a youngster like me was expected to do.

"You there—" Momose said, turning toward me, "what's your name?"

"Ijichi, sir."

"Not your *surname*, you fool—don't you know nobody calls himself by his surname in our business."

"Eiji, sir."

"And what do you want to do with yourself?"

"That's the trouble—I haven't made up my mind yet."

He grinned. Then, out of the blue, he said: "How'd it be if you became a gambler?"

"A *gambler*?"

"Don't look so surprised! Listen: if you ask me, you've got the face of a yakuza, not an honest workman."

"Now you say so," put in Tokuzo, "you *might* be right at that. We hold a session here sometimes, and I can tell he's got what it takes. I've often thought so myself."

Momose took out a long small-bowled pipe and stuck it in

his mouth. His deputy, who was just behind him, promptly came up with a light for him. He took a good drag at the pipe, then blew the smoke out through his nostrils, staring at me all the while.

"Something about your face tells me you're not going to stay here. Once you get stuck in a place like this, you could be here a hundred years and never get anywhere. Every man's got his own nature, which decides what he's best at. The guys in this place were cut out to be raftsmen. But with someone born to be a yakuza it wouldn't work out, and I've got this feeling you weren't made for the straight and narrow."

I hadn't had any idea of becoming a professional gambler till then, but once it was put to me it seemed right, somehow. So I bowed and said, "Thank you, sir. I hope you'll arrange things for me as you see fit."

Momose nodded. "In that case, I'll see what I can do. There are reasons why I can't have you at my place, but luckily there's an outfit called the Dewaya whose boss is a pal of mine. I'm sure he'd be willing to take you on."

About a month later, with this gang leader as my sponsor, I joined the Dewaya as an apprentice yakuza.

It was the day of the Boys' Festival, in May 1924, when Momose took me there. The boss of the Dewaya lived in the center of the entertainment district of Asakusa, just behind the street where all the little sushi shops were. This was after the Great Earthquake, of course, but new buildings were already going up—not any of those temporary shacks, either, but properly built shops as you might expect in Asakusa. The whole area was humming with activity—I suppose they'd call it a building boom nowadays....

In spite of the terrible fire, the Sensoji, the great Kannon temple, was still standing, undamaged. Everything round about was burned flat, but the temple buildings and the things in the grounds had survived. According to what people said, great waves of flame had come blasting toward the temple any number of times, but, each time, a breeze sprang up and the fire changed direction. More than a hundred thousand people had taken shelter there, all of them watching with their hearts in their mouths. When the fire finally moved away, they cried for joy; said it was Kannon's doing, and went down on their knees. The day I went to join the Dewaya, there was still a great crowd of people come to worship there. And I remembered Sei-chan the bricklayer, and what he'd said about the blessings of Kannon....

Anyway, the place my new boss lived in was a perfectly ordinary house, you'd hardly have noticed it was there at all; but when Momose took me through with him to the back of the house, we found the boss waiting for us in an impressive-looking room with a fine old charcoal brazier, just like something in a period movie.

The two men said all the usual polite things to each other, then Momose told him all about me.

"So there you have it," he said when he was finished. "I hope you'll do what you can with him."

The Dewaya boss, who was wearing an expensive kimono of handmade silk, folded his arms and took a long, hard look at my face.

"Right, brother—it's a deal. I'll take charge of him and do my best to make something out of him." He looked really dignified as he said it; and, then and there, I decided that it'd be a privilege to work for him.

His name was Yamamoto Shuzo. I've had a long life, but of all the yakuza who've made it to the top, I've never come across a finer man than him. He was strict with himself and with others, but basically he was a kindhearted person, open to other people's feelings, and very popular in Asakusa. Most people seem to think that all yakuza are bums; but for someone to become a boss it takes more than just muscle or brute force. Otherwise, any old fool could make it. What's important is to have the kind of qualities that make the guys under you loyal to you—ready to die for you if necessary.

The boss of the Dewaya

It's easy enough to talk about it, but it's not half so simple in practice. The Dewaya was a genuine, top-ranking gang that was known everywhere, but it kept itself strictly out of the public eye. The boss's house, for instance, belonged to the owner of one of the sushi shops on the main street, and at New Year's and the Bon festival the boss would go personally to pay his respects to the landlord. He was never short of money, but it was typical of him that he'd never have used his money to force a neighbor to sell him his place.

The Dewaya made its living, of course, through gambling. Yakuza nowadays are mixed up in all kinds of things—in the construction business, drugs, real estate, loan-sharking, you name it—but it wasn't like that in the old days.

The yakuza's real trade was gambling, and nothing else. In my day, if a yakuza made money some other way, people would look down on him. "Oh, *him*," they'd say. "He's trying to have it both ways. Goes scrabbling after a few extra yen because he can't make a proper living from gambling, he's not good enough at it. He's a fraud, that's what he is."

A boss didn't have as many men under him as he does today, either. All he needed was some guys to run the games and enough others to guard his territory—a few dozen at the very most. The Dewaya's territory covered the area around the Asakusa Kannon, the rows of shops leading up to the temple, and over behind the International Theater, so it was one of the best bits in Tokyo. Still, there were only five or six of us who hung out at our home base, and about thirty altogether when you included those who had their own places and came to our joint as necessary.

The gambling joint was on the other side of the alley from the house. To look at, it was just like any other housing in that area, but as it didn't look respectable to have a lot of men traipsing in and out all the time without doing any actual work, the people in the neighborhood always called it the "scenery store."

There were lots of small theaters in Asakusa. You need a lot of scenery and props to put on a play, and the Dewaya was officially supposed to make the scenery. And there actually were all kinds of backdrops and stuff stacked in a corner of the joint. It was only a cover, of course; nobody did any actual theater work.

When it got dark, they brought the dice out. I was only an apprentice, so I wasn't allowed in on the games. An apprentice lived in, and was made to do the dirty work; it was a way of testing how tough he was, and whether he was really suited to the yakuza life.

What did I actually do? The washing, the cleaning, the cooking, and the shopping. Besides that, I had to get on good terms with the local tradesmen, and help keep the streets in the neighborhood swept and clean. That kind of thing.

The Dewaya didn't have any maids at all. That meant that the rookies had to do everything there was to do inside the house. I used to wonder at first why they didn't employ any women, till one of the older men called Shiro explained. He'd been the most junior one there until I came, so now that I'd turned up he was inclined to throw his weight around.

"Here—" he'd say, staring hard at me out of his big square face, "think what happens if there's a police raid and you get caught. They ask you who was running things, what kind of people came to play, how much cash was involved, and so on. A guy with any guts would rather die than give anything away, but you can't expect the same of a woman."

According to him, women couldn't ever be trusted in our line of work.

"What I mean is, basically they're weak. They might say they'd never spill the beans, but just strip them and get to work on them where they're sensitive, and all their good intentions go by the board. They end up talking—and that's the end of the organization. That's why we don't keep any women here and do everything—I mean everything—our-selves."

Besides Shiro, there was another lad just above me called Shunkichi. He was a good-looking guy, with a good brain too; the boss put a lot of trust in him. Once I'd started working in the gambling joint, it was Shunkichi who really coached me in the various rules the yakuza had.

There were detailed rules for almost everything—the way you greet the people above you and below you, the way you talk to them, the way you show you're listening to them—everything. It's a feudal sort of world, quite different from ordinary life outside. It even affects your personal relations with women.

"Never get mixed up with a decent girl," Shunkichi told me. "People would cut you dead for it; he's a jerk, they'd say, he doesn't have the money to pay for a woman and he doesn't do his work properly—that's why he runs after nice, respectable girls....

"Suppose, too, you kept making trouble for people outside our business, d'you know what would happen? You'd be handed your walking papers. I mean, you'd be driven out of the brotherhood. And once a yakuza is disowned by his boss, there's nowhere left for him to go. Japan's not as big as you might think—you'd be out in the cold....

"The most important thing in this business is guts. A man without guts just doesn't get anywhere. Men are like the timber they use to build a house with—there's the kind of wood that forms the main pillar supporting everything, and there's the wood used for the paneling in the john. Without guts, you're always going to be the underdog: you'll stay a rookie. On the other hand, if you've got real guts, you're going to be treated with respect—not just by other yakuza, but by the police as well."

Shunkichi was always saying that the crucial thing for a yakuza was to keep himself in a strong position.

"Ask yourself, now, how the Dewaya manages to keep its territory in Asakusa. You want to know? It's because anybody can tell right off that this is an outfit to be reckoned with. There are lots of places in this area where people come to eat and enjoy themselves, so you get a good class of customer at our games. Naturally, there are other yakuza who'd like the area for themselves. So you see, if you aren't powerful, somebody's going to come barging into your turf. And if you can't shove him out again, you've had it. So you mustn't ever show any weakness.

"Suppose you get into a fight with a guy from some other gang: whatever happens, you've got to squash him. If you let yourself get hurt without hurting him back, then it doesn't matter what happens to you, *we're* the ones who're going to suffer.

" 'Look at that,' people will say, 'a guy from the Dewaya got worked over and he's taking it lying down—I didn't think they'd sunk so low.' So it's a rule that you give as good as you get.

"If you lose, you're either dead or in a hospital. And if you win, you go to jail—that's the kind of life it is. Either way, if you get into a fight, you've got to make sure you win. Still, so long as you handle things properly yourself, there's no need to pick a fight in the first place; after all, it's the customer that's the important thing, and if you get so scrappy that ordinary people get scared of you, you're going to scare your customers away too.

"So it's like they say: the good hawk hides its claws. You've got to be on your guard, of course, but as far as possible you should take the ordinary people round about into account. That way, word will get around among the locals that the Dewaya rookies are a decent crowd."

I took all this to heart, and in the year or so I spent working in the kitchen, I was careful not to show off or act superior with the young assistants in the shops I visited, who knew I was with the Dewaya. The same went for the door-to-door salesmen I met every day.

A street seller

The first of these to come in the morning, of course, was the fishmonger. In the old days, they caught masses of sardines in Tokyo bay in the winter. There's an island in the mouth of the Sumida river—the place I escaped to with Kenkichi and his girl after the earthquake—and almost everybody there was a fisherman. By the end of that year, things had settled down again, and the wharves were jammed with so many barrels of sardines there was hardly room to walk. The wholesalers and fishmongers used to take their pick of them, then go around selling the stuff in buckets slung from a pole across their shoulder. This was while it was still dark, so they'd sing out as they walked: "Sar–dines. Sar–dines!" And people would call out: "Over here, please!"

We were a big household, so I usually bought a hundred or

more at a time. The fish were absolutely fresh, with their scales all silver and shining. Not a bloodshot eye among them.... Sometimes we'd pound them up in a mortar to make dumplings to go in a soup for a kind of sardine stew. Good it was, too. Sometimes we'd have them raw. You pulled on their guts with your fingers so that they came out evenly, then took off the heads with your fingers too. Then if you stuck your thumb in between the flesh and the skin and pressed along gently, the skin would come off clean without using a knife at all. You couldn't do that if the fish weren't fresh, but these were only just caught, so it was easy. Then you'd slice them up thin and eat them dipped in soy sauce. That was good too, I can tell you!

"Where'd you learn how to do that?" one of the senior guys used to ask me as he stood there watching.

"At the timber foreman's place."

"Did you, now.... Not bad, considering."

There was a maid at Tokuzo's house who'd been there for ages, and she it was who taught me how to get the skin off. To her surprise, I got the hang of it immediately, and did it by myself, as smoothly as that, from then on. So I became the sardine specialist.

They used to catch a lot of black squid, too, and whenever some good stuff came in, the fish man would come straight to us, seeing as we were one of his best customers. With black squid, you eat the thick parts as sashimi. The legs you chop up small, sprinkle with salt, and leave for several hours to make *shiokara*, to go to with saké. Just put some of the *shiokara* you've made that morning on a bowl of rice with your supper, then pour hot tea over it and shovel it down with your chopsticks—it's delicious. They used to get gobies in as well, big ones—these were best made into tempura. The biggest ones,

83

with a lot of fat on them, we'd grill on a charcoal brazier and eat with a bit of salt. Poor people, incidentally, used to have goby as a special treat on New Year's Day.

Boss Yamamoto wasn't all that strong physically, so he was fussy about what he ate. He was specially fond of soup with small mussels or clams in it, and whenever I made it he'd come back several times for more. The clam man only came on his rounds up till around cherry-blossom time. That was the spawning season; from then on, all the goodness went into the eggs, so the flavor deteriorated. That was why clams in the cold season were so special.

Once they'd had breakfast, all the older men would go off to work, leaving me to clear things away and deal with the day's various callers—not all of them tradesmen. Sometimes, for example, a wandering monk with a great long-nosed goblin mask on his back would come chanting prayers. I say a monk, but he was really just a beggar, and you could never actually hear the words of the prayer he was mumbling.

The same kind of monk had often turned up at Tokuzo's place too, but if I gave them any money the maid there would always bawl me out. "What are you wasting your money for?" she'd shout, right there in front of them. She was the sort of woman who gets her kicks from always finding fault; you couldn't really like anything about her. With the Dewaya, though, it was very different: the boss was forever telling us to be polite whenever possible. So I generally gave them a copper or two, even if they came every day, and whenever a real beggar showed up I used to wrap up some leftovers—rice-balls, or a bit of fish—for him.

Either way, the old-style yakuza were always concerned about their reputation; relations with the neighbors were important to them, and they made an effort to be civil with

84

people, whoever they were.

Getting on for two years after I joined the Dewaya, I was given permission to sit in on the dice games, but only a few months later there was a police raid, and I was sent to jail. I'll get to that in a minute. Just before I got nabbed, though, something so unexpected happened you'd think it was part of a play.

One of the regulars at our games was a man called Matchan. He was about seven years older than me, with the sort of tough good looks that women really go for. As a player, he was the world's worst—never had any luck at all. He told us he had a tobacconist's shop, but I've no idea whether it was true or not. For some reason, anyway, we took a fancy to each other.

Before long, he invited me for a meal at his place, which was in an area called "Cannon Flats," on the other side of Tsukuda. People say it got the name because the mud washed down by the river collected there to form a shape like a cannon, but it also seems that long ago they used the place for testing guns. There were quite a lot of big buildings there compared with Fukagawa, but the part where Matchan lived was a huddle of small houses.

I found that Matchan was living with a woman—not bad-looking, either. It was around lunchtime when I got there, and the food was already set out on the table, with saké to go with it.

"Make yourself at home," said Matchan, and the woman started pouring me a drink. We chatted about this and that, and were just beginning to enjoy ourselves when we heard a woman's voice out in the hall saying, "Hello, is there anybody in?"

I had the feeling I'd heard the voice before. Matchan's friend got up and went out. We could hear their voices: "Hello, there! What's that you've bought?" "An octopus—a whopper, isn't it?" "I'll say! But come on in."

Dangling the bag with the octopus in it, she came back right away with another young woman behind her. I took one look and nearly had a fit. The visitor, too, went as still as a statue. You wouldn't believe it, but it was the judge's mistress I'd known back home.

It really *is* a small world. It turned out that Oyoshi, as she was called, was the other woman's sister.

Well, after that the four of us had a meal together. The thing that surprised me most of all was how little Oyoshi had changed. According to her, though, I myself had changed a lot. Either way, meeting her again now, more than three years after I'd followed her to Tokyo, those days back in Utsunomiya seemed like something out of a dream. She was still the judge's mistress, she said, and was living in Shinagawa.

"Anyway," said Matchan, "Eiji's a young man with a bright future in the Dewaya, and you've got your judge, so it'd be safer for you not to get too involved again." He was half teasing, but he looked a bit worried all the same. Oyoshi, though, was the picture of innocence.

"Eiji's bound to have someone else he's keen on," she said, giving me the glad eye all the time. "I'm sure he's forgotten all about the likes of *me*." She was just as sexy as she'd been before; it was enough to make your toes curl.

I met her three more times after that. But then we were raided at the gambling joint and I was put inside, and after I came out I kind of felt I was a proper yakuza now, and never went to see her again.

Resisting the Law

As I was saying, the first time I was a guest of the government was when I was nineteen. It would have been around the end of autumn; Okada, one of the older men, had got together about thirty guys in the joint behind the International Theater, and they were playing as usual when all of a sudden a whole crowd of policemen came bursting into the place.

"Don't move!" they yelled—enough to put the wind up anybody, it was. In this situation, none of the people playing are going to put up a struggle. It'd only mean a stiffer sentence, so the sensible thing to do is go along quietly. You keep an eye open, of course, for any chance of slipping out, but once you're sure there's no escape the best thing is just to let them arrest you.

In my case, though, this was my first raid, and I felt like a fight. I suddenly got an idea, and gave a hefty tug at the light hanging from the ceiling. There were a lot of sparks, and the room went pitch-dark. It was as if you'd stirred up a hornets' nest. The cops put on their flashlights, but they weren't much use; everybody cleared out, and the only people caught were six or seven customers.

The next day, a local detective turned up at our base.

"Look," he said to the boss, "as you know, we raided Okada's place last night. But some bastard blew the fuse, so the whole lot got away. I want you to send whoever was responsible along to the station."

"Right...," said the boss. "If that's how it is, I'll ask my boys about it straightaway. If it was one of them, I'll hand him over. Just give me a bit of time, will you?"

"OK, make sure he comes, then," the detective said, and left.

So the boss got everybody together and told them what was up. "The cops are going to look bad if they make a raid without nabbing anyone. I hear it was you, Eiji, who cut the lights, wasn't it?"

"That's right."

"They won't be satisfied if *you* go along. They came to get Okada, and they're going to get mad if just a kid shows up instead. But we need Okada to run things at his place. What d'you suggest we do?..."

So I shuffled forward on my knees—we were all sitting Japanese-style in front of him—and bowed and said: "I'd like you to let me go."

"You really mean it?" the boss asked.

I bowed down to the floor again and told him I was ready and willing.

"I see ... I suppose we *could* leave it all to you. But with this kind of thing I'll have to ask the others." He turned toward Okada first: "You've heard what Eiji says—how do you feel?"

"He's still a kid," Okada said, "but he's got what it takes. I guess it'd be OK." So the boss checked with another of the senior guys called Muramatsu, one of his right-hand men.

"I reckon he won't let the side down, whatever happens," he said.

That convinced the boss.

"Eiji," he said, "it's up to you how things turn out for Okada. Go and show them what you can do."

And that settled it. I was happy, you know. I really felt on top of the world as I went off to turn myself in at the police station.

The police were a bunch of arrogant bastards in those days. The way they talked to you, for a start, was real rough. The older men had already told me a lot about them, but hearing and actually experiencing are two different things. The minute I showed my face, it was: "And what the hell brought *you* here?" I mean, you can tell from little things like that what you're in for.

I gave them my name. "It was me that was running the game last night," I said. "I won't make any trouble, so just deal with me as you think fit." I'd been taught that bit by one of the old hands.

"Well, you've some nerve, turning up here all bright and cheerful like this. You might learn to regret it," one of them said, staring hard at me. "Wait there," he added, and went off to fetch the detective in charge of the case. The detective looked pissed off as soon as he laid eyes on me.

Another detective, a fat one with a moustache, came in after him, and this one hit the ceiling.

"You say *you* ran the game?" he yelled. "Who put you up to that, then? Come off it! What d'you think this place is—a nursery school?" I expect he wouldn't have minded so much if I'd been a bit older and better known.

"Listen, kid," one of them said in a menacing kind of way. "We keep files. We know how the Dewaya operates—and you're small fry!"

"The little bastard fancies himself a real yakuza," the fat guy put in. "D'you think we've got shit for brains?" he shouted, and gave a great thump on the table. Quite a nasty sight, he was.

I took a good look at their faces. I'd been prepared for the worst, but these were really ugly customers. Still, I wasn't going to say, "I'm sorry, actually it was one of the senior men called so-and-so who ran the session." I'd sooner have died.

So I stuck to my guns: "It's like I said: just go ahead and question me." That made the fat dick *really* angry.

"Right," he said, "we'll just have to make your body talk a bit."

The interrogation room had a tatami floor—quite big, about ten mats, I'd say. There were a few other people—petty thieves and pickpockets—being questioned in the same room. The detective at work next to us was grinning. "A real pain in the ass, isn't it?" he said, knowing what was coming next.

"Hey!" the fat cop called out to one of his staff. "Bring us a dozen sticks here, will you?"

"Coming right up, sir," was the reply.

They tied my hands behind my back and hauled up my kimono. Then, when the sticks arrived, they lined them up on the tatami and sat me down on them bare-assed. It wouldn't have been so bad if the sticks had been smooth, but these were split into triangular shapes, with sharp edges.

"Well, how's it feel? Does it hurt? You hear me? I'm asking if it *hurts*." The detective kept slapping me around the face as he spoke.

"I see ... a tough guy, eh?" said his partner, and bared my back.

"If you're going to come clean, now's the time," he said.

He was an old hand at interrogations, and he knew where it hurt. Really good at it, he was. He never hit your head or your chest. No—he aimed for the soft places around your buttocks and thighs. It hurt, but it didn't break any bones, so he could lay into you as much as he liked.

Before long, though, he realized that he wasn't going to get anywhere just beating me.

"How about this, then?..." he said. And they took turns standing on my thighs. My backside was directly on top of the sharp part of the sticks, so with a grown man standing on my thighs the sticks bit into the flesh till the blood came. As if that wasn't enough, a couple of them rocked me backwards and forwards, singing out "see-saw, see-saw" as they did it. I'd been gritting my teeth, trying to put up with the pain, but that was more than I could take, and I couldn't help crying out loud.

One man went on steadily rocking me; occasionally, he'd run a hand over my head and say "Quite a guy!" I hung on grimly, till suddenly I found myself lying there on the floor, wet all over. I'd fainted, and they'd poured cold water over me.

"Don't think we've finished with you yet, you creep," the fat detective said, and got on my thighs again. And they began singing out "see-saw, see-saw" again. To say it was agony wouldn't describe it. Fatso was grinning like an ape: "He's tougher than he looks, this guy," he said.

One thing I ought to explain is that with gambling at least—I don't know how it was with other offenses—the police only used torture on the yakuza, and not, as far as I know, on the customers. The point is that your average customer, who wasn't used to this sort of thing, would spill everything at the first hint of violence. But then in court he'd say: "I only confessed because they tortured me; it was all a pack of lies really—I was forced to tell them." And if he had a good lawyer to plead his case, the man in charge of the investigation might well get the boot. So generally speaking they didn't put too much pressure on non-professionals.

You might wonder about the yakuza themselves—whether *they* wouldn't give the police away like that in court. But they weren't such fools. If they had done, they'd have paid for it afterward. The cops would have spread the word: "That one's a sneaky bastard. He got two of our men transferred. So we don't need to look the other way any more." And they'd stake out the gambling joint and keep a twenty-four-hour check. That way the regulars would be too scared to come anywhere near the place, and it would just die a natural death. You see, if the police ever wanted to put the squeeze on them, the yakuza couldn't have made a living. So, however rough their methods were—even if they half killed you—you never let on about it at the trial. And the cops, on their side, knew they were safe however much they put you through it, so they could afford to let themselves go.

With the yakuza, keeping your mouth shut when the screws were really on counted as a kind of medal. Not just with the other guys in your own mob, either: it was talked about by the police, who began to treat you as a proper yakuza, and in other gangs, too, so that someone who stuck it out got a reputation. But if you couldn't take it and confessed, that got around in the same way. "Him?" people would say. "He *sounds* like the real thing, but inside he's all soft, like a bit of rotten tofu." You got a label put on you, and people avoided you. Once that happened, you were finished: you could stay a yakuza all your life, but you'd be down there at the bottom all the way.

I was well aware of all this, so I kept my lip buttoned, and the detectives got the message: I was the kind who'd never knuckle under. That suited me fine, and they put me down in their report as the one who'd set up the session.

Next, I was taken to court. The judge at my trial took a look at the police report and said "Is this correct?" and I said "Yes, sir, it's correct," and I was sentenced to three months in jail. The upshot of it all was that I went off to Sugamo prison feeling fairly proud of myself.

There's a world of difference between today's jails, which are meant to reform you, and the ones I knew, which were there to punish you. You'd done something wrong, and to pay for it you'd got to suffer: that was the general idea in the old days. Worst were the warders, who'd absolutely no human feelings, no sympathy. We've got absolute control over you, body and soul—that was their attitude to the prisoners.

The prison uniform was a red kimono. You know the color they paint the gateway to a Shinto shrine? It was that kind of red. You were lucky, though, if it was the proper color still—in most cases they were all washed out, and patched all over into the bargain. The cloth itself, too, was worn so thin you might have been wearing a mosquito net. I mean, if you looked you could see right through it....

It was the coldest time of year when I went in, so they gave me cotton underwear and socks. Apart from that, there was a single quilt to sleep on, with a blanket, and a box with a bowl for putting rice in, a bowl for beanpaste soup, and a metal plate.

I was put in a big cell holding twelve men. In those days they still had the prison boss system, so I got on my knees at the entrance to the cell, bowed right down, and gave a formal greeting. And one of the men who'd been there longest spoke up from the back: "You look pretty young, but you'll find it's not too bad here when you get used to it, so mind you keep on good terms with everybody...."

Anyhow, that was the way I went to jail.... But you know, I must have been a bit bigheaded or something, because there was a brawl the very first day I was in, and I got charged with "insubordination" and had a rough time of it.

As soon as I sat down in one corner of the cell, a hunched-up guy next to me started muttering things about me. He had a gray, dirty-looking complexion, and half his hair was white, though he couldn't have been much over thirty. His teeth were a dark yellow and his breath smelled of bad eggs. I didn't know what had pissed him off, but he pitched into me without warning.

"What's your name, eh?" he began. "Your name, I said!" The way he said it was really mean. Seeing he was set on picking a fight right from the start, I naturally got worked up myself. Shunkichi had told me before I went in that it wasn't done to ask too much about other prisoners' affairs.

"You see," Shunkichi said, "we're different from ordinary criminals. For us, it's an honor to go to jail. But the rest of the poor bastards have just slipped up somehow and been put through it by the police, then bullied by the courts, and finally locked up. That's about it.

"So your ordinary offender wants to have a bit of peace and quiet, in jail at least. He wants to forget all the unpleasant things that happened outside and take it easy for a while. So it's a rule inside that you don't ask other people all kinds of things about what they did outside. If someone feels like talking about himself, it's OK, but otherwise it's better not to ask."

Shunkichi had been in Sugamo himself a couple of years earlier, so I was all ears. I'd assumed that everybody I met in jail would be like he said; but I don't know why, this man next to me really got on my nerves. I put up with it for a while, then began to lose my temper, and in the end I shouted at him:

"Look, mister, with all respect, why don't you just shut up."

"Say that again!"

"I mean, you keep cackling like an old hen."

I suppose anybody'd be annoyed by that. Anyway, he went pale and got to his feet.

"You bastard! You know what happens to people who say things like that around here?"

He grabbed the collar of my kimono and yelled "Get up!" So I put a twist on his arm and threw him. He let out a great yell. That brought a warder at the run, and he clapped some handcuffs on me on the spot. Didn't say a word to the other man, though, who just sat there sneering at me.

"What've I done wrong?" I yelled.

"That's enough! You keep quiet!"

It really wasn't fair. I just didn't understand why the warder took the other fellow's side. It didn't stand to reason. I sprawled out in the corridor with my legs and arms out, and the warder tried to drag me away by the handcuffs.

"Come on, get up, you awkward bastard!" The warder called another of his mates, and they hit me across the face. Then I was dragged up to the second floor.

They make prisons so that everybody can always see what's going on. As I was hauled upstairs, the prisoners in the cells round about were all watching, holding on to the bars like monkeys. One loop of the handcuffs was taken off my wrist and fixed to an iron bar in the floor. "Let's see his ass," the warder said, and his assistant pulled my kimono up to the waist. Next the warder told him to tie my legs together, so he bound my ankles to another iron bar with a rope so that they'd got me on all fours, unable to move at all.

"You won't look so pleased with yourself when we're finished with you. We haven't had any trouble here for a long

95

while, but look what happens as soon as *you* come in. I'm going to beat a bit of sense into you!"

You just can't imagine what punishments were like in prisons then. Police torture was an amateur affair, but in the jails it was really professional—in a different league altogether. The police, after all, were supposed to be interrogating a *suspect*, but once you were inside you were a condemned criminal, so they didn't need to hold back. And since dealing out stiff punishment was the warders' business, they showed absolutely no mercy.

I was wondering what they were going to beat me with, and it turned out to be a rubber hose, a six-foot length of the stuff. It really did the trick, too. It's far more effective than hitting you with a hard stick. When it whacks against your ass, it bites into the flesh and snicks a bit out as it goes. I've put up with all kinds of pain in my time, but they don't come much worse than this. You sometimes see slaves being whipped in movies, don't you? Well, nobody who hasn't actually experienced it can come close to imagining what it's really like. If you have, the sound alone's enough to make your skin crawl and your hairs all stand on end.

When it comes down thwack across you, you feel it's ripping out the marrow in your bones, and your head reels right to the core. And everything around you goes black for a moment. Those warders were experts at finding just the right spot to hit. When they hit you across the back, the end of the hose curled around your belly and sliced the skin like a razor blade. The blood oozed out. All the same, I didn't think it'd look good to make a noise with everybody watching, so I kept a desperate grip on myself. I counted up to fifteen strokes, but the rest I was past thinking about.

It was all I could do to stop myself groaning out loud. As

the hose came whistling through the air, the pores all over my body gave a kind of shudder. When it landed, it felt like it had smashed the bone. So I hung on desperately to the metal bar—but then it came whistling through the air at me again. The sound of bombs coming down during the war wasn't anything compared with that. There must have been a lot of men who died in prison that way.

I suppose it was being young that helped me get through it, but, all the same, when they finally let me go I could hardly breathe, even. It hurt too much to lie down, so I sat upright all night. When I leaned against the wall, it was like my bones were crying out. I spent three days like that, sitting up, but then it gradually got better and I was able to lie down again.

Even so, what happened to me had its advantages too. I mean, after the beating, the other men looked at me in a completely different way from before. I hadn't called out, however much it hurt, and they treated me with a new respect. Even the guy who'd got me into trouble in the first place said he was sorry in quite a humble way.

II

From the end of January on into the middle of February, the man was confined to his bed almost completely. He had a persistent cough and a low fever, and I was afraid that he might get pneumonia if something wasn't done about it. So I suggested that he go into a hospital for a while, just until the fever disappeared. But he obstinately refused. "Don't worry," he said, "it'll get better eventually if it's going to." The woman who was nursing him said much the same. "It's no use once he's made up his mind," she told me, "so if it's not too much trouble perhaps you'd drop in occasionally and take a look at him?"

I had never spoken to this woman until the man took to his bed. Her name was Hatsuyo, and I was told she was his wife—whether the second, or third, or what, I wasn't sure—but you could tell from a glance at her face that she had originally been in the bar or restaurant trade. I'd already been visiting the house for some months, and spending hours there at a time, but not once had she put in an appearance. It gave me the uneasy feeling that she'd probably prove a very difficult sort of person. When I actually met her, however, she was surprisingly straightforward.

She would bring in cakes and tea, for instance, and make some remark such as "I must say, doctor, you seem to have plenty of time to spare. If you go on visiting a dump like this every evening, people are going to start saying I've got a lover."

So I would sit by his bed, listening to what he had to say, till he slowly began to recover; then, sometime after mid-February, he was finally able to get up and sit with his legs in the sunken hearth again.

Sea Bream

I'd done my three-month term in jail, and it was the evening of the day before I was due to leave. The governor summoned me and gave me a talking-to. "I know the sort of world you're mixed up in," he said, "but if you commit an offense again, don't expect to get off as lightly next time. So try to keep your nose clean. Tomorrow morning, I want you up at four, ready to move out."

That shook me. "Four o'clock's a bit *too* early, isn't it?" I said.

"No," he told me. "I called your boss, and he said a lot of them would be coming to meet you. But the locals won't want a crowd of gangsters standing around in front of here, so the earlier the better."

Being still under twenty and a new boy in the gang, I didn't think it was very likely there'd be much of a welcoming committee at all, and I still felt that four o'clock was going a bit far. But I was wrong. When I came out of the prison gates carrying my belongings, with a warder to see me off, I couldn't believe my eyes: there must have been seventy or eighty men waiting there for me. Even the boss himself had turned up specially.

It was pitch-dark and cold enough to make you shiver. But they'd split open a bale of charcoal and got a whole line of fires burning cheerfully along the prison wall. I just couldn't see why they'd laid on such a homecoming for a kid like me.

As I walked toward the boss with my head bowed, first one then another of them called out to thank me. I remember he was wearing a black silk kimono and a cape with a boa collar around it, and as I came up to him he said,

"Thank you, Eiji, you did pretty well." Then he took a closer look at me. "Well, I'm pleased to see you looking fairly fit," he said, "and not any thinner." At the sound of his voice again, the tears suddenly came into my eyes.

"At this rate," his deputy, Muramatsu, said with a smile, "you'll be a real man in no time now."

"Here, Eiji—" said Shiro, "change into these." I took the cloth bundle he gave me and went up close to one of the fires. I wrapped the long loincloth tightly round and round me and put on the kimono, which was one of Shiro's old ones.

The welcoming committee, outside Sugamo jail

The first thing I did after that was go to the boss's home in Asakusa and pay my respects to him properly.

"I'm glad you came through all right," he said. "Good work."

Boss Momose looked in, too. "I was worried," he said, looking pleased with himself, "seeing I'd recommended you to the Dewaya myself. But it's turned out OK."

Muramatsu added his formal thanks, then handed me an envelope with more than two hundred yen in it. "This is what you made while you were on the job," he said.

You might wonder what "on the job" meant, but in our world, you see, serving time in jail is considered a kind of work. So they make a point of putting your money by for you while you're inside, and handing it over when you get out.

After that, on a different day, there was a "coming-out party" for me. I was obviously pretty junior in rank, so they could hardly have had it in too classy a restaurant, but it was on the second floor of a sushi shop right by the Asakusa temple; and, as the main guest, they put me at the top of the table close to the boss, with the other heads of the gang on our right and left. There were some quite high-up members sitting down there near the bottom of the table, which made me feel uncomfortable. And the food! I mean, one of the dishes laid out for me was a great sea bream a good foot long, on a fancy plate.

Before we dug in, I went up to the boss, bowed down with my forehead on the tatami, and "reported for duty," so to speak. Then I did the same thing with each of the older men in turn, who thanked me again. After a while, the boss called me over.

"You've had a rough time," he said, "so take it easy for a while—don't try to do too much. You've got to think of your health. Why don't you go to a hot spring or somewhere and rest up for a bit?"

He took a big paper packet out of the front of his kimono.

"They all chipped in to give you this present. And here's a list of people who contributed; make sure you take care of it.

"Listen," he went on. "You're going to find yourself relying on these people one way or another all your life from now on. Mind you don't forget your obligations, because it would let *me* down if you didn't...."

In our line of business, this sense of obligation to the people you were connected with was incredibly strong, I'm not exaggerating. I took the list of names, and always kept it by me from then on. As for the money I got from the boss, though, I'm afraid it all went on gambling and visits to the red-light district long before I got around to going to any hot spring.

So I enjoyed myself for a while; but there's an end to all good things, they say, and one day without warning I got a letter that gave me a nasty shock. Believe it or not, it was from my father's place in Utsunomiya.

When I opened it I got another shock: it said a notice had come for me to go and have an army physical, and I was to go home immediately. I'd assumed the old man had washed his hands of me long ago, so it put me on the spot, having a letter suddenly turn up like that. Even so, I could hardly ignore it, so I went and talked to the boss. The boss took a hard look at me.

"I see...," he said, taking things in his stride. "You *look* grown-up too—I'd assumed you were about twenty-five or -six. Thought you were past the call-up age."

"What should I do about it, then?" I said.

"There's only one thing you can do," he answered. "Go straight home and put your father's mind at rest. You're lucky to have both your parents alive. The best thing would be for you to follow in the family business. After all, you don't *have* to be a gambler, do you? So get off home and do your duty by your family!"

And without any more ado he arranged a farewell party for

me. So I said goodbye to the older men and went back to Utsunomiya.

I found that both my grandparents had died some while back. My mother cried when she saw me.

They did the physical at the town hall. There was quite a crowd of other guys there taking it too, but what surprised me was that only three out of all the men examined in the Utsunomiya district were given a grade A, myself included. That would never have happened later, as the Pacific War got closer. You see, it was 1926 when I went for my checkup, at a time when people were still feeling fed up with war. The First World War had started in 1914 and gone on for four years, and everybody felt tired of fighting and everything to do with it. There'd been a lot of disarmament conferences, and the trend was for big cuts in battleships and weapons and troops.

My father felt a bit better about things when he heard his son was one of the few people in all Utsunomiya to make the A grade. Some of the neighbors actually sent around a box of "red rice" to congratulate the family like they used to. That was as far as the good things went, though; not two weeks after I'd passed the test, along came my call-up papers. I was to report for duty with the 75th Infantry Regiment on such-and-such a day in December. The 75th was one of the units policing the northern part of Korea, so things didn't look too promising.

There was no Manchukuo yet in those days, which meant that Sakhalien and northern Korea were as out-of-the-way as you could get in Japan. Korea of course had been annexed about twenty years earlier and was Japanese territory.

Anyway, that was the place I was supposed to go and guard. The time for me to leave wasn't far off when an invitation came from the Veterans' Association—which meant, mostly, retired army officers living in the Utsunomiya area—saying they were holding a send-off party for us and would I be kind enough to attend. And, sure enough, they put on quite a show, with a crowd of old men in beards and uniforms with lots of decorations dangling on their chests, all of them there specially for us. Seemed we were to go in a bunch to visit the local shrine. A lot of ordinary townsfolk came along with us, and what with the banners they carried and the rising sun flags, you'd almost have thought it was some big festival. Anyway, off we went in fine style to pray at the shrine in the center of town, like we were *heroes* or something....

Leaving for service overseas

Troops in Kimonos

When we actually left to join up—now, that was a real send-off. The whole station was crammed with people. We weren't wearing uniforms, though, but kimonos: all three of us in cheap everyday kimonos with capes over them and wooden clogs on our feet. We didn't have any belongings with us—no cases, no bags, nothing but a bit of cash and a cotton towel tucked away in the front of our kimonos. The army had told us they'd supply us with everything we needed when we got there, so we set off in the clothes we stood up in.

We got to Osaka sometime after noon the next day, and the day after that left harbor in a six-thousand-ton freighter bound for Korea. There were hundreds—maybe thousands —of conscripts on that boat. Meals consisted of riceballs and pickles, that was all. A temporary john had been set up on deck; the other ones below decks couldn't keep up with the demand, so they built this big boarded affair up top. You had your crap, and it slid off straight down into the deep blue sea....

We arrived in Korea, and some of the new recruits left the ship at Wonsan. The ship couldn't be brought alongside the cliffs there, so the troops went ashore by lighter. The rest of us stayed on board and went on to a place called Unggi, in what's North Korea nowadays. It was the harbor closest to the Soviet Union, with Vladivostock, the biggest Soviet naval base in the Far East, not so far away. It was a fishing port, a desolate kind of place, population three thousand at the most, I'd say. I could only see a few people dotted about here and there. The wind off the sea was bitterly cold—it was December, after all. There must have been about a thousand of us who'd come on this far.

Well, they got us all neatly lined up, and an officer strutted out like a toy soldier to give us a pep talk.

"This here is the northernmost outpost of the Japanese Empire," he said. "You men, as soldiers, have been entrusted with the great responsibility of guarding one of the nation's frontiers. I want you all to bear this in mind, and carry out your duties to the very best of your ability...." And so on, lots more of the same stuff, his moustache bristling all the time.

None of us recruits had been abroad before of course, so we were completely lost. We just knew we'd been brought to a pretty godawful dump, and we felt jittery, though we tried not to show it. On top of it all, it was hellish cold.

The speechifying went on and on, and people were beginning to mutter that they'd freeze to death if they were kept standing there much longer, but it came to an end at last, and everyone was issued with special overcoats against the cold —great loose-fitting things made of fur, cut big so you could put all kinds of things on underneath without making them tight. They were really warm, and everybody sort of came to life again and cheered up.

We were also given fur hats. I think they were made of dog fur, anyway they were all stiff, and they covered you up leaving just your face peering out. We looked at each other when we'd put them on, and laughed and fooled around like a bunch of kids. But then a train arrived, and we were ordered on board.

I say train, but it was more like a toy railway, huffing and puffing along through the hills with smoke pouring from a tall smokestack. Wherever you looked there were mountains —bleak-looking mountains, with the rock all bare. They went

109

rolling on, those bare mountainsides, up and down, up and down forever, with nothing but the odd shrub growing here and there. The grass was flattened down all over. There'd be mountains and a valley, more mountains and another valley, getting gradually higher all the time. Not a house to be seen. We went on through this for hours. "God, what a place," we sat there saying to each other in low voices. "You wouldn't even catch bandits living in a hole like this!"

Eventually, the transport officer came around again and said, "We'll soon be arriving in Komusan. But you lot are going on further, so make sure you don't get off the train."

It was getting dark outside. Komusan was a miserable spot, enough to send chills up and down your spine. The recruits who'd got off there were each handed a rifle and ammunition. Then they all formed up again, an order was given, and they marched off the platform and out into the dark.

Being raw recruits, of course, they didn't actually have any idea how to fire a gun. Only a few days before, they'd been farmboys or shop assistants, and this was the first time they'd so much as laid hands on a rifle. But off they marched, these troops in their baggy coats over their kimonos, with their ammunition bound around their waists, and rifles on their shoulders. A long line of them, straggling on, then disappearing into the darkness....

We started off again, but it was night now and you couldn't see anything. There was just the sound of the train—clickety-clack, clickety-clack. The seats were wooden, and the backs too, so there was no question of sleeping. Right there in the middle of the coach a stove was going, glowing red-hot. In those days, any amount of coal was to be had in the mountains in the north of Korea, so they weren't mean with it. A soldier was shoveling the stuff up and stoking the fire, making a steady clanging noise.

I was tired out and kept trying to get some sleep, but I was too keyed up, and the seat hurt my butt, so I stayed half-awake, half-asleep all night. The faces of the soldiers sleeping around me looked like children's. But then, all of a sudden, everyone was woken up by the NCO yelling. His voice sounded quite different this time; it was as though a dog had turned into a wolf overnight.

"Rise and shine!" he bawled. "We'll be at our destination soon. Now, you don't want to disappoint your officers and the other soldiers already there, do you? So I want you on your mettle. Standing up tall and straight, right? None of your shivering and looking cold. Got it?"

His voice had had plenty of practice after years in the army, and it rang all the way down the coach. There wasn't anyone left asleep when he'd finished.

Dawn came and we arrived in Hoeryông. About eight o'clock, I'd say it was. There was a thin layer of snow on the station platform. It was a small, miserable-looking station, with just one wooden building standing there on its own. There must have been about five hundred of us left by this stage, and everyone was looking around as if to say what the hell are we doing here?

But almost at once an order was barked out: "Fall *in*!" and we all formed up in two lines, and moved outside. And there, in front of the station, drawn up in ranks, were the troops sent from the regiment specially to meet us, around sixty of them in all.

"To the new recruits—sa-*lute*!" someone shouted, and the guard of honor gave a smart salute, all together. You never saw anything so overdone in your life, it was like something on the stage. You'd wonder how they managed to strike poses

111

like that, like a bunch of Kabuki actors. Not a muscle twitching. I took another look, and I could see the officers' moustaches were all frozen, with icicles hanging from them. It made their eyes seem to bulge all the more. Their faces, too, were quite different from soldiers I'd seen back home, they gave me quite a shock. I wondered if troops trained in the cold always got that fierce sort of look.

They'd already decided which of the new men were to be assigned to which unit, and an NCO from each company came forward and read out the names. As your name was called, you stepped forward and lined up. When the number was completed for each company, the NCO reported to his commanding officer: "Company recruits all present and correct, sir." In due course, a sergeant bellowed an order, and the troops who'd come to meet us marched off in front, boots crunching along the icy road, with us slipping and slithering behind them in our wooden clogs. First one then another of the men would fall on his ass, getting bellowed at in the process:

"You there—what d'you think you're up to? Get a move on!"

You had to feel sorry for us—we were like prisoners of the Red Army being led away. The road was wide, and went on for miles, white all the way. There were houses lining both sides but not a sign of life in them.

It was on December 20, 1926, that we got to the regiment, if I remember rightly. The place where it was stationed was literally the most northern point in Japanese territory, with Kilin province, Manchuria, next to it in the west and Soviet Siberia in the northeast. Between Korea and Manchuria on the one side and Russia on the other ran the Tuman river.

112

This froze over so thick in winter that you could drive a horse and cart across it. The base was on the outskirts of the town, with an embankment all the way around it. Beyond the embankment there were fields as far as you could see, then gently sloping hills. At the foot of the hills was a training ground. But it couldn't be used till spring; during the winter the training was done in an open space called the "barrack square," inside the base itself.

As soon as we arrived, we were given the usual pep talk, then issued with our kit and equipment. This included uniforms, but I weighed about a hundred and ninety pounds and was six feet tall, and there wasn't anything my size in No. 2 Company, which I was posted to. They immediately got the tailor to alter one to fit me, but it wasn't ready in time for the next day, so I turned up for the colonel's address in the same clothes as before: a kimono with a fur coat over it.

We all lined up in the barrack square, with a company commander in front of each company and the battalion commander in front of *them*—three companies to a battalion. The senior officers looked like old men, their moustaches all frozen white.

One at a time, the company commanders would report to the battalion commander:

"No. 1 Company—its commander and a hundred and so many men!"

Each report was greeted with a salute and a "Carry on." When this was over, the colonel rode over on a horse and stopped in front of the battalion. He had a fine moustache and a row of medals on his chest.

The battalion commander then shouted out:

"No. 1 Battalion—its commander and so many hundred men!"

As he shouted, he raised his sword in front of his face. The colonel returned the salute without saying anything. It looked impressive, but they did the same thing again, and again, with each battalion in turn. The more time went by, the stiffer your body got. The recruit next to me had gone as white as a sheet around the forehead and gills and was shaking like a leaf. I was thinking that the skin under my nose felt a bit tight when I suddenly realized there was an icicle hanging down from my nose.

The colonel got up on a stand and began his address.

"I am your commanding officer, Colonel Kuga," he started off, up there on his pedestal. Everything in sight was covered with ice, so his voice carried well. Very dignified he was, with the medals glittering on his chest, and his peaked cap. "You are all soldiers of the Empire, specially chosen from among its citizens. You should consider it a great honor...."

Honor, my ass! I was too cold to worry about that kind of thing. Even if you tried to stand still, your body started trembling of its own accord, and your arms and legs felt like blocks of wood. My feet were a bit more comfortable than the day before, as I'd changed from clogs to boots with a fur lining, but under my overcoat I was still wearing the kimono, and an icy breeze came blowing in between my legs. I'd bound gaiters around my bare legs, but that was worse than useless in weather like that.

"The 75th Regiment, to which we belong, has the privilege of defending the very front line of the Empire. Beyond us lies not a single unit of friendly forces. This gives us a very special role to play, and I want you to respond to the great hopes our nation pins on us by devoting every possible moment to training yourselves, physically and mentally, to become the kind of troops that will serve as models etc. etc...."

114

On and on he went with his fine words. But suddenly the soldier next to me tilted to one side and fell flat on his face. His body was as stiff as a frozen tuna fish. The squad leader and a private picked him up and carried him off to the infirmary on their shoulders. That seemed to set things off, and soon another two or three men collapsed in another company. From their faces, you'd have thought they were dead. It would have been a bit better if we could have stamped our feet or waved our arms about, but we weren't supposed to move at all, and it was no wonder people froze. I was just beginning to hope they'd take me to the infirmary myself, when all of a sudden the talk ended.

"To the commanding officer—sa-*lute*!" someone bellowed. The guy in charge of No. 1 Company had his parade sword high up in the air.

"Eyes—*right*!" He had an impressive voice, I'll say that much for him.

"Not that way! Right! *Right*!" a sergeant was shouting, and I could see a man looking to the left. That's the army for you —they even have to tell you how to move your eyes!

Once No. 1 Company had finished, it was our turn to salute the colonel, and when we'd all finally had a go, the colonel went off on his horse, still stiff as a ramrod, back to headquarters.

I heaved a sigh of relief, but then a new order rang out:

"To the battalion commander—sa-*lute*! Eyes—*right*!"

And we had to go through the whole rigmarole again, company by company, till all the senior officers had pushed off. If we hadn't, at long last, been ordered to dismiss, we'd all probably have frozen to death.

The next day, instead of pep talks, they had us jogging around the parade ground. Dozens of times, "*left, right, left, right*," with our rifles on our shoulders and knapsacks on our backs. And all the while, they bawled at us: "Don't slouch, there ... keep your cap straight"—breaking us in, like horses.

Four or five days had passed when training was suddenly suspended. The Emperor Taisho had died; it was December 25. I remember it well because they told us the whole regiment was going to pay its respects at the exact time that his remains left the palace in Tokyo. A sergeant briefed us:

"You're to wear the cleanest underwear and socks you've got, and you're to shave, clean your teeth, comb your hair, and shine your boots. You can wear gloves, but not greatcoats. There must be no more talk than is absolutely necessary, and, even then, keep your voices down. No running in the corridors. Get your supper early, and go about it quietly."

We all got ready and waited, then around eleven at night the order came to assemble on the barrack square. We trooped outside in the dark—and immediately started shivering, of course; it would've been bad enough even in thick furs. After a while, each company was told to light a beacon, using firewood they'd already got out of supplies; quite high piles of it, in bamboo frames. Once these got going it was a lot brighter, especially as the ice around them reflected the flames like a mirror. In fact, the whole parade ground stood out like it was broad daylight, though it was pitch-dark where the light didn't reach. The fires crackled, and the red flames blazed up into the sky.

"Eyes—*right*," we heard, and the colonel appeared, armed with another speech: "It is with a deep sense of awe that I have to inform you that His Imperial Majesty passed away at 1:25 this morning...." The colonel didn't have a greatcoat on, either, but he was "setting an example." Anyway, when he was done, we all turned to face east, and bowed low. On the stroke of midnight, a bugle played. And went on playing. The inside of my nose had been frozen for some time, and with each breath I took you could hear it crackling. But the bugle stopped, and our company of loyal, shivering troops filed back to our barracks.

If there was one thing about the army that was better than jail, it was the food. The number of men in the forces had gone down thanks to disarmament, so there were plenty of supplies. We got our three meals a day, and something to eat in the middle of the afternoon as well—all kinds of different things, every day. One time, they doled out five big chestnut buns each. Besides that, we sometimes got sweet bean soup or *butamame*. There'd be three big rice cakes in the bean soup. *Butamame* was a kind of pork-and-beans stew—and they gave us a whole plateful of the stuff.

On Sundays, we could go off base. There were shops in the town, and eating places too—most of them run by Koreans, but two or three run by Japanese as well. And then there were the usual brothels, of course.

These were bunched together in a sort of small-scale red-light district. Most of the whores were Korean women. They also had quite a few White Russians, since this wasn't long after the revolution there. I guess some of them couldn't make a living any way except by selling themselves.

As for money, we got twenty-two sen a day—two yen twenty sen every ten days. That was about twice the pay soldiers back at home were getting. It was more than enough to buy food with when you went off base—I mean, a bowl of noodles was just five sen. But it didn't go far in the brothels, except maybe at the cheapest ones. A woman who was anything like decent cost a lot. So you had to choose between spending twenty days' pay on a single night or eating out for quite a while, which wasn't easy. But just around that time I got a sudden windfall. The boss of the Dewaya sent me a letter with twenty yen in it.

"Apart from getting a new emperor," it said, "things haven't changed much here. Asakusa's as lively as ever, and everybody keeps busy enough. Just make sure you don't get sick. The money I'm enclosing isn't much, but you'll be able to buy yourself something decent to eat with it. I'll send some more when it's gone." I was so pleased with the letter, I took it to bed with me that night.

I never got to spend any of the money, though. Our letters were censored, and the company commander was told about the cash.

"Ijichi—what do you think you're going to spend this money on?"

"I was thinking of getting myself something to eat, sir."

"You mean army rations aren't good enough for you?"

"No, sir, it's not that, it's just I thought it'd be nice to eat in town once in a while."

"There's far too much money here for you to use. I'll keep it for you till you're discharged."

I didn't have any say in the matter, and I didn't see the money again all the time I was in Hoeryông. There was a White Russian girl in one of the brothels who was a real beauty, and I'd hoped to get something going with her, but I never managed it in the end.

The Cage

There was talk of tigers being seen over in Komusan; in
Hoeryông, we had wolves. One night, I was on sentry duty,
about three months after I was drafted. I was standing with
the hills right in front of me, and a moon shining bright and
white, and suddenly I heard a wolf howling somewhere up
there on the ridge. I looked up and saw the slope of the hill
to the east shining silver all over. It was bare—Hill 294, they
called it.

I looked carefully, and I could see a small shape standing out quite clearly against the snow at the top of the hill.
It was howling at the moon. "Yeow, yeoow, yeoooow ...," it was
going, dragging it out. It made your hair stand on end.
When they heard it, the pigs and chickens who'd been grunt-
ing and clucking in the farms round about all suddenly
stopped, just like that. Dead silence. Before long, several more
shapes turned up alongside the first one on the ridge. Then
the number doubled and trebled till there were too many of
them to count—and the leader started coming down in this
direction.

There was a deep gully between Hill 294 and another
slope. Well, they followed that gully down. I'd already heard
that the wolves were attracted by the rubbish dump outside
the north gate of the base, and it seemed that was what they
were after now. They came to scavenge there when they ran
out of food up in the hills.

Before long, the pack reached the bottom of the gully and
headed straight across the frozen fields, with their leader out
in front. I had my gun, of course, but they kept coming on

quite steadily, so I didn't feel too happy. The other sentry and me were still wondering if it was all right, and whether we shouldn't alert the sergeant, when the wolves came right up to us.

It's funny, you know—the wolves on their side seemed to know that we weren't going to fire our guns without good cause. If this wasn't the case, they'd hardly have had the nerve to come right up close like that. In the end, this great pack of wolves was only about thirty yards away. Then the leader and what seemed to be his followers started eating, with one of them, a tough-looking brute, acting as a sort of guard to keep an eye on us. By now, Sergeant Sugano had got wind of what was happening and came creeping up with three men to have a look, but though one of the pack was still keeping a wary eye in this direction, the rest went on busily eating without paying us any attention.

I don't know how long this lasted, but in the end the leader stretched his head up into the air and howled—"yeow, yeoow, yeoooow ..."—and the whole mob suddenly stopped what they'd been doing, just like that. Some of them must have wanted to go on eating, but I suppose they're a bit like our own gangs, and the boss's word is law.

The wolf bringing up the rear kept looking back as they scampered off. They really had things well organized, those wolves; the sergeant and the rest of us just stood there marveling at it. Ordinary animals wouldn't stand much chance against the likes of them. It's not so much that wolves are strong, it seems, as they're intelligent.

The pack got gradually farther and farther away up the gully, till they disappeared altogether. We watched, thinking we might see them again at the top of the hill, but they didn't show up, and we never saw them again that winter.

Well, we got through the winter. Spring came, the grass started growing, and suddenly we were in trouble. I mean, training began in earnest. Up to then, we'd been having basic training on the barrack square, but once it got warm real training started outside the base, at the foot of the hills. Seems the colonel had got it into his head that he was going to put the 75th Regiment through its paces till it was a match for any other regiment. So the officers gave us a pretty rough time. We were being bawled out all day long. I got really fed up.

Come the end of summer and I couldn't stand it any more. So I got the idea of deserting. It makes me smile to think about it now. I don't suppose anyone who wasn't alive before the war would understand just how serious an offense desertion was in those days. The deserter himself was shot if he was caught, so for him that was the end of it; but it made life really tough for his family afterward, at least out in the country anyway. People just cut them dead. The son was a traitor, so his family were "non-citizens," and no treatment was too bad for them. So nobody with any sense at all would ever attempt it. And the people back home, as well, would almost rather their boy got killed than have him desert. But in my case—well, I wasn't exactly the "sensible" sort, and I was considering it quite seriously.

Still, talking about deserting was all very well, but there was no chance of getting back to Japan proper, so it meant getting away to another country or nothing. The quickest and easiest way would be Manchuria. Manchuria was only just across the Tuman river.

Luckily enough, just around that time, I was assigned to the rifle works, where they repaired all the regiment's weapons. A couple of likely looking men were selected from each company to see to the company's own weapons, which meant there were about twenty of us in the workshop. Rifles were fitted with bayonets at the muzzle end, but the bayonets themselves weren't usually sharpened; they had to be sharp if you were going into action, though, so we were taught how to use the grinder on the blades in case of an emergency.

The best things about working there were that you didn't have to run round and round the parade ground, and you could talk to the other men. In other places, you couldn't ever say what you liked because an NCO always had his eye on you, but here nobody bothered you so long as you were doing your work. The noise of the machines helped keep things private, too. That was convenient—particularly when I struck up with two guys from the machine-gun unit there, Nemoto Yusaku and Kanazawa Ryukichi. Kanazawa was a schoolteacher's son, and knew a good deal about China. I don't know who he got it from, but to hear him talk you'd think he'd been there himself.

There was a general feeling in Japan in those days that anything was possible if you went to Manchuria. I remember a popular song that went: "I'm setting out, so you come too, / To a nobler, freer fate— / Across the seas to China where / A land and people wait." Anyway, the fact was that Manchuria was a mess. The place was crawling with warlords, bandits, and so on, who did more or less what they liked—I mean, there wasn't any proper government, so it was every man for himself, and a lot of people who couldn't make a living in Japan drifted over there hoping to get rich. A fair number of them became bandits, apparently. There was a woman called

"Okiku of Manchuria," for instance—she was one of the best known—who was supposed to be a force to reckon with there, with at least five thousand followers of her own.

All this was happening just when we were being trained in Korea, so I felt it mightn't be a bad idea to set up as a bandit myself. At first it was me and Kanazawa and Nemoto who worked out the plan, but after a while we decided to include two others, and started thinking of ways of stealing machine guns.

The reason I liked the idea of us becoming bandits was that I'd actually seen some myself. I told you there was a red-light district near the base, didn't I? Well, once every few months or so, the leader of the most powerful mob in Kilin province used to turn up there. His name was Wang Kungtê, a big, dark man with a long moustache drooping down to his chin. He wore a bearskin hat, and his hair hung down his back as far as his waist. He used to come riding in on a fine chestnut horse—not a care in the world—with about a dozen armed followers, then spend a couple of hundred yen there in a matter of two or three days, before heading back across the Tuman river again.

I saw him several times myself, and I always thought what a fine sight he was: riding along with his hair streaming out behind him in a great clatter of hooves, and his men all galloping after him with the tails of their coats flapping in the wind. Compared with us, all smeared with sweat and dust from the parade ground, you'd have thought he came from a different planet. Seriously, I'd have given anything to be like him, galloping off as far as I could get from there!

I only found out later, actually, but it seems Wang Kungtê wasn't the kind of man we imagined. He had ties with the Japanese secret service; the reason he came to Hoeryông was so he could sell Japan information about the situation in Kilin. They had an agreement, apparently: officers from the Special Service Agency would have a secret meeting somewhere with him, listen to the latest information he'd collected, then pay him off. That's why he was able to come to the brothels right close to our HQ, bringing his followers with him and passing our sentries on the way. But we, of course, hadn't the faintest idea about that in those days, and just went on waiting for the right moment to escape.

Luckily or unluckily, though, the time never did come. As the day for putting the plan into practice got closer, Kanazawa began to get the wind up, and ended up confessing to the sergeant. So we were all arrested and interrogated. According to the sergeant, the others owned up without any fuss, but I swore I didn't know anything at all about the plan. So they treated me as the ringleader, on the grounds that I was holding out on them.

Soldiers who'd committed some serious offense were usually sent to the military jail at Kokura in southern Japan. I was resigned to the same thing happening to me, but instead they put me in the regimental lockup.

This was located behind the sentry box at the north corner of the base, a square, concrete building. The door was a wooden grille, like Japanese jails in the old days. Inside, though, it would have put Sugamo to shame. It was really small—a kind of kennel just big enough for one person to get into. You couldn't stand up or sit down, you had to lie down all day. It was two feet wide, just enough to take your shoulders, and roughly two feet high and seven feet deep, with a wooden floor and one blanket. It was almost impossible to turn over.

The other guys had all been put in the same sort of holes, but there was hell to pay if you talked, so generally it was quiet as a tomb. About the only thing to look forward to was when you went to the john. There was a john inside the lockup, and they took you there twice a day. You can't piss only twice a day, though, so when you wanted to go you had to call the guard.

"What's the matter with you?" he'd say.

"I'm sorry, but I've got to have a piss."

"Well, you can't. You can wait," he'd tell you, sharply.

"Please!... Please!" you'd try again, and after a few times, grumbling, he might let you go.

The other men asked to go in the same way several times a day, so the give-and-take between the guard and the prisoners, and the sound of footsteps, at least made something to listen to.

Anyway, I just can't tell you how tough it is, not to say boring, to stay lying down without being able to move. Particularly after the first few days, when the others were let out and I was left there all alone, it was plain agony. If you leave a person cooped up in the dark for too long, he begins to go funny in the head. It's worse than any torture. You know you'll be bawled out if you shout, but you just can't help calling, "Please ... please—let me out for a minute to stretch my back a bit." But the guard would just bang on the bars and yell, "That's enough of that noise there!" If you still went on hollering, he'd open the door and clip you around the head. The result was I gradually went a bit balmy, and began to spend all my time cursing Kanazawa and telling myself I'd kill him.

I had all kinds of dreams too; one of them I can remember quite clearly. I was galloping along all by myself on a horse, and I suddenly realized I was Chinese. So I got in with a group of bandits, and was riding about the plains when another group came riding toward us on red horses. Funnily enough, the red horses weren't real ones, they were rocking horses. And the strange thing was, the rocking horses were much faster than our own. I was wondering why that should be, when someone said to me, "Don't you know? This is the age of rocking horses, not real horses any longer." Then I realized it was Kanazawa. "You fucking traitor," I thought, "I'm going to kill you!" and I chased after him, but he turned around to look at me. "D'you think a Chinese can beat a Japanese soldier?" he said, and he laughed out loud. The next thing I knew, he had a machine gun and was coming after me. I ran like mad, till I found myself on the parade ground with men pounding around it in single file and the colonel shouting orders at them. I looked harder, and saw he was just like Nemoto.

"Nemoto—what are you doing here?" I asked.

"You're a traitor," he said. "I'm going to have you shot!"

They grabbed me on the spot, and tied me to a tree in the middle of the square. I was so cold I didn't know what to do. Everything all around was white with snow. I knew I'd die if I didn't do something. "Help!" I yelled. There was a sound like thunder over my head, and I woke up and found the guard beating on the grille with an iron bar....

So time went by in much the same way, day after day, till in the end I got delirious. According to the guard, it was on the twenty-fifth day that they finally let me out. When I first went outside, the bright sunlight and the crowds of people made me giddy. The main thing I noticed, though, was that the world looked completely different from what it had before I was put inside. I suppose I'd lost all my kid's illusions and

126

begun to see things straight. Even when I bumped into Kanazawa again, I didn't feel any particular hate for him at all.

The training grounds, which I couldn't stand the sight of usually, looked wonderful to me then, and the hills and countryside were like a dreamland. Yes, the lockup's a dreadful place....

Alexandrias

I was in Hoeryông for something over a year after that, but nothing much worth mentioning happened.

I was discharged at the end of 1927. I celebrated it by drinking all night in the red-light district. As we were sailing east on the ship, Japan came into sight, a line of green hills; my eyes got damp, and I stood there gazing and gazing at it. We played cards for cash to kill time on board—games organized not by a soldier but a professional gambler. Quite a few of the men were completely cleaned out, and had to send a telegram from the ship: "Please meet at Osaka with money." When I was discharged, they'd given me back the twenty yen the boss had sent me, and I used it to make a hundred and seventy-five yen in all.

My mother and sister were at the harbor in Osaka to meet me. We stayed in Kyoto that night, then did some sightseeing the next day; I bought a couple of bolts of best Nishijin brocade for my sister to have a kimono made, and a kimono sash for my mother. That was the first and last time in my life I did the decent thing by my family.

I went home to Utsunomiya and loafed around for ten days or so. During that time the local Veterans' Association gave a party to celebrate my return from army service—just as if I was a hero or something; I was tickled pink. But before long a letter came from Okada, one of the senior men in the gang. I knew he was the type that hardly ever wrote letters, so I felt a bit uneasy and opened it in a hurry.

"The boss has got something wrong with his chest," he wrote. "He's getting treatment, but things don't look too good. You're one of us he's been specially good to, so why don't you come and see him?"

That was a real shock. It was some time since I'd got back, but so far I hadn't even dropped in to see them, and I'd been thinking it was about time I went and paid my respects. So I hopped on a train that day and went to Tokyo.

The boss was really pleased to see me safe and well. He noticed how the training had made me thinner, and teased me about it: going into the army had made me half as handsome again, he said. He seemed better, in fact, than I'd expected; it set my mind at rest for the moment. When I thanked him for the pocket money he'd sent, he said I could make up for it by telling them about life in Korea. So I told them how I'd been put in the lockup.

That interested them a lot. They all knew what it was like to be in jail, but nobody'd ever been in a military lockup before. I'd seen something even the older men hadn't seen, and that made me the center of attention, I suppose. When I told them how I'd tried to desert they were disgusted. They made fun of me, said I ought to have known better than to trust someone who was a clever talker, and that I must have gone a bit soft in the head.

With one thing and another, I ended up staying on in the Dewaya, and never went back to Utsunomiya at all.

Well, things went on all right for a while, and then the boss took a turn for the worse again. It was the beginning of summer. He wasn't bad enough to go into a hospital, but they told him he'd got to rest, so he went off to stay at his villa on the coast at Oiso. With Muramatsu taking charge of the games, there was nothing for him to worry about. I mean, Muramatsu was famous as a gambler, there wasn't a single yakuza in Tokyo who didn't know about him. So the boss could afford to recover in his own time. Once a month, Muramatsu would send him some spending money, and if anything else came up he'd send down one of the younger men.

One day he called me in and said it was my turn to go and see how the boss was getting on. "Right," I said, "I'll be off straightaway." But he gave me a lot of instructions before I left. "Listen," he said, "the people who live in Oiso aren't your ordinary locals. The big political and company bosses have all got fancy villas there; if you get into a quarrel or make any other sort of trouble, it's the boss who'll suffer for it, so mind what you're doing. And you can't go looking like that, either. Put on your best clothes, and go and get your hair cut good and short."

It sounded a bit funny, coming from him, but orders are orders, so I went and got myself trimmed up. Then, when I was ready to leave, he gave me some money and said, "This is to buy a present for him. Go to Sembikiya in the Ginza and get some Alexandrias to take with you."

I hadn't a clue what Alexandrias were, so I asked him. He said they were grapes.

You know, in those days, in the late 1920s, almost nobody ate things like that. I imagine they grew them in greenhouses or somewhere; most ordinary people, though, would never even have *seen* them. Muramatsu handed me twenty yen to buy them with. I couldn't believe it.

"But—how am I going to carry as many as that?" I asked.

He laughed. "You stupid bastard," he said, "you've no idea what things cost, do you? Listen—just go along to Sembikiya and ask for twenty yen's worth—you'll find you only get a handful."

"You're kidding!"

"Stop messing around and go and see for yourself."

So I went to Sembikiya, still only half believing him. But it was just like he said: all I got for my money was two measly bunches. I was so worried about squashing them, I kept them in my lap all the way down to Oiso, feeling like I was holding the crown jewels....

The boss's place was a solid-looking house with a big garden. The garden had an artificial hill and a pond in it. Beyond it, I could see a grove of pine trees. And beyond them was the sea.

"It's been a long time, boss," I said. "How are you feeling?" He looked pleased to see me. He'd got a tan, so you'd never have thought he was sick. I handed him an envelope I'd been given for him.

"Muramatsu said this was to keep you going for the time being." He nodded. "And these are a present—I bought them at Sembikiya on the way here."

He thanked me, and Shiro, who was helping out at the villa, went and washed the grapes, then brought them back on a dish.

"Boss," I said, "these grapes are something special, aren't they?"

"What's so special about them?"

"But they cost twenty yen!" I said, my eyes fixed on them. Shiro too was staring at them with a sort of half-starved look.

The boss laughed. "Haven't you ever had them, then?"

"No."

"Didn't you get them in Korea?"

"Even the colonel probably couldn't afford things like this."

"I don't suppose he could. Army officers are all moustaches and empty wallets." He chuckled. "Here—try one, for the colonel's sake."

131

I hesitated, so he said "Go on."

So I picked one grape and popped it in my mouth.

"Good, aren't they?" he said.

"I've never had anything like it."

"Well, have another."

"You sure?"

"Go ahead. It's more fun watching *you* eat them." So I helped myself to another grape. Shiro was positively drooling as he watched all this.

"You want some too, Shiro?"

"Well, I wouldn't say no."

The boss was grinning, and the grapes sat there on the white dish like bunches of jewels.

I went to visit him any number of times after that. Maybe he was worried in case I was stopped and questioned by the police, as he didn't much like it if I went out to look around the neighborhood. Anyway, the other villas there were all as quiet as the grave, even in daytime; the only sound you heard was the wind in the pines. Rich people actually seem to like lonely places, but not me—give me a crowd, every time.

That summer, though, things started to look up. The doctor had been to visit the boss one day, and I'd gone to see him off at the gate, when I saw this girl walking in our direction from the beach. She had a parasol, and was wearing a lovely summer kimono, and there was an elderly woman with her who must have been her nanny. The girl glanced at me as she went by, and her face was so pale and pretty it looked almost transparent. But she'd gone a few steps past the gate when a car came around a corner on the other side. As it went whizzing past, it brushed against her parasol, sending it spinning to the ground. The girl had a hand up to her forehead.

"What's wrong, miss?" the nanny asked her in a worried way.

I ran over to pick the parasol up, then looked at the girl. Her face was as white as a sheet.

"She doesn't look too good," I said. "I should take her straight home if I were you."

But the old woman was in too much of a flap to be any use, so I told her I would help.

"It's not far," she said, "—just over there, where that big pine tree is."

Since the girl didn't seem up to walking, I offered to carry her on my back. When I picked her up, though—well, it came as a surprise: not just how light she was, but how nice she smelled. She was obviously high-class; in fact, I found out later that her family was related to Egawa Tarozaemon, the scientist who built a special furnace for making some enormous kind of cannon.

Anyway, you won't believe me when I tell you this, but the girl took a fancy to me. The nanny came every day after that to fetch me. I'd hear her voice calling for me at the entrance, and Shiro would go out to see her, then come back with a big grin on his face.

"The young lady would like the honor, Eiji," he'd say, kidding me. So I'd ask the boss if I could go, and—bad-temperedly, telling me not to stay too long—he'd usually agree.

On the way over, the nanny would ask me things about myself, how I spent my time. And I'd fob her off with something like, "I don't work, but I dabble in the theater now and then." The bit about not working went down well, you know. Most rich people don't do a stroke of work, they live off the fat of the land, and it seems she thought I was the spoiled son of some wealthy family. Another thing was, I'd been sort of toughened up in Korea, so I expect I seemed different from the other young men-about-town. Either way, she swallowed the story whole.

"Mr. Ijichi is in the *theater*," she told the girl, all goggle-eyed, when we arrived.

"How nice. And what kind of plays do you appear in, Mr. Ijichi? Foreign ones?"

"Oh, I'm just a dabbler," I said, "not a real actor." Since I didn't know a damn thing about the theater, I *had* to say this in case they asked me any more questions.

It was a big place they lived in, but apart from the girl the only people there were the nanny and two maids and an old gardener. Sometimes a piano teacher and a man who looked like a university professor dropped by. But as for where her parents were, or how long she was going to stay, I'd no idea. Whenever I went there, the whole place was neat and tidy, not a speck of dust. Through the windows you could see a fine Western-style garden, with an old-fashioned cannon standing on a rock.

The girl sometimes suggested a game of cards, so I joined in, but all we played was Sevens—no betting at all; it was a complete waste of time as far as I was concerned.

They asked me to go to the beach with them, too, and we went, all three of us. There was a small cove, and people from the villas were swimming. There were men in red loincloths standing around on the beach as well, and others sitting on the rocks, all staring hard at the people swimming.

I asked what they were doing, and the old woman said, "They're keeping watch to see the young ladies don't drown." They were hired for the summer, she told me, just to keep an eye on them, one for each family. I don't know how it got that way, but those lifeguards all wore the same red costume.

On the beach in Oiso

The girls who'd finished swimming came up the beach, each with a guard in tow carrying a parasol over his shoulder and a basket. The men had deep tans—they looked almost black against the blue sea.

"Shall we go?" the nanny said, and the girl and me walked side by side along the sand toward the house. On the way, she kept giving me little glances from under her eyelashes, but every time I looked back she glanced away again. She seemed to want to say something, but couldn't because the other woman was right behind us.

It went on like that for days, with us doing the same things over and over again. I couldn't work it out: a couple of youngsters, boy and girl, going for walks on the beach with a chaperone, and *nothing happening*. It seemed unnatural. Still, she was as pretty as a picture, just the right age, and a type I wasn't used to, either, so you couldn't really say I didn't enjoy it.

135

One day, we got back to find a pile of Alexandrias on the table. More than ten bunches there were, and beside them was something that looked like a watermelon, only it wasn't. I was wondering what it was when the old woman asked the maid who they were from.

"They sent them over from Mr. Dan's place," she said. That was Dan Takuma, the father of the famous composer; one of the big shots in the business world—Mitsui, or was it Mitsubishi? His summer bonus alone would have been a couple of hundred million in today's money. Even our boss couldn't have matched that.

The nanny offered me a grape, but I was still puzzled by the watermelon. When I tried it, it was as sweet as honey, sweeter than the grapes ... and that was the first time I ever remember having muskmelon.

Anyway, not long afterward, the boss told me to go back to Tokyo. Didn't even tell me why. But I had a good idea what was on his mind, so I said goodbye and took the first train into town. And I never saw the girl again, never even went to Oiso any more. The boss had told Muramatsu not to send me. And, on my own side, I wasn't interested in meeting the girl in secret—the worlds we lived in were just too different.

Eloping

A couple of summers after that little holiday, Muramatsu sent for me and said:

"Eiji—I want you to go to a brother's place in Funabashi to help him out. There may be some trouble, so I'll give you ten men to take with you."

There was a boss called Ito Chiyokichi over in Funabashi, in Chiba prefecture, he told me. Ito's gang had had connections with the Dewaya for many years now, and both sides had a strong sense of obligation to each other. Lately, though, Boss Ito had being coming under pressure from a new-style yakuza called Yahagi who'd been getting uppish, and he was in a fix. So they'd decided that this Yahagi ought to be taught a lesson, and they'd asked the Dewaya for reinforcements.

"If the other side wants a showdown," Muramatsu said, "then let them have it. Any time you want more men, just let me know."

"Leave it to me," I told him, talking big. "We'll take care of things, don't worry."

You don't know how pleased Boss Ito was. Gave us the red-carpet treatment—made us feel like VIPs. After all, without us he'd have been in danger of losing his territory. So no expense was spared: the best geisha in town, parties every night.

Being entertained like that, we naturally felt we owed them something in return, and if Yahagi's people had wanted a fight we'd have taken them on any time. We were on the lookout for them—but there wasn't a cheep out of them. Which wasn't surprising: basically, they were just a bunch of hicks, and as soon as they heard reinforcements had come from Tokyo, all the wind went out of them.

"It looks as though things have worked themselves out," Ito told me, "so why don't you stay on for a bit and have some fun?"

I got the feeling somehow that he didn't really want a fight, that he'd be happy so long as he broke Yahagi's hold on the entertainment area. Kamezo, my junior in the gang and a close friend of mine, was fed up about it, though; Ito was a slob, he said. But only having come there to help out, it wasn't for us to meddle. So we decided we might as well take it easy, and just loafed around town every day.

The place we were staying at was right in the middle of the red-light district, a lively spot. There were cafes, and places serving Western food. One of these Western restaurants was called Byodoken, and it served sweet things too, like shaved ice with syrup. I was going past one day—a really hot day it was—and the sight of the banner fluttering outside with "Ices" on it made me suddenly decide to go in.

I sat myself down and said "Give me an ice, will you, any flavor," and was wiping the sweat off my face when I looked up and there behind the counter was this girl, a real stunner. She had her hair done up and a striped kimono on, with a white apron over it. I went there again the next day, but it was lunchtime and the place was crammed. When she saw me, the girl smiled and said "Hi—you're back then!"

She was bustling about attending to the customers, making the other waitresses look invisible. There was something I really fancied about the way she moved. Her forehead was wide and a nice shape, and she had fair skin and almond eyes, with a friendly expression. Her arms as they stretched

138

out of her apron sleeves were slender, and had a sort of glow to them. I sat there in my seat and just stared and stared at her as though I'd gone soft in the head. I went the next day, too, but it was crowded again.

"Hot weather we're having," she said with a little smile in her eyes. I hung on in my seat, and before I realized it the place was empty and the girl was sitting over in the corner.

"What's the time?" I asked.

"Three o'clock!" She had a tray held against her chest. Her hair threw a shadow on her cheeks, which had skin so fair you could almost see through it, and she had rather full, red lips.

"You got anything against people who don't do regular work?" I said.

"You're one of the Dewaya people, aren't you?"

"I won't come any more if it bothers you."

"The owner's a bit scared."

"Then I shouldn't be here, should I?"

"You know the cafe over there on the corner? Wait for me there."

And that was how I struck up with Omitsu. But it wasn't long before Ito got wind of our affair and sent for Kamezo to pass on a warning to me.

"I want you to tell Eiji," he said, "—that girl is connected with Mr. Makuta. There'll be trouble if he gets mixed up with her."

This guy Makuta, he told Kamezo, was the right-hand man of a certain Mr. Omiya, and quite a big shot locally. Omiya was a construction boss well known at the time in the Kanto area; anybody in the yakuza world would have known who you meant if you mentioned him. According to Ito, Makuta was hoping eventually to set Omitsu up as his mistress.

"You've got women on the brain," Kamezo told me. "The boss was complaining about it only the other day."

"It's different in this case."

"I'm not so sure. It seems pretty much the same to *me*."

"Give it a rest, will you!"

"The boss won't like it if he hears, you know."

Kamezo was genuinely worried for my sake. So I decided to have it out with Omitsu, and arranged to meet her at a cafe.

"Are you hitched up with a man called Makuta?" I asked, right out.

She shook her head, putting a spoonful of ice cream into her mouth, then sat there gazing at me.

"I'd be in trouble if it got around that I stole somebody else's girl."

"It's all right. Honestly. I mean, he's got a wife."

"Has he, now...." That gave me a better idea of how the land lay. It was hot that day, you know; the sweat poured off you even when you were sitting still. There were little beads of sweat standing out on her forehead and her hairline.

She took a handkerchief out of the front of her kimono, then stretched out her hand and wiped my forehead.

"What shall we do?" she said.

"About what?"

"Us."

"You're crazy, that's what you are."

"I suppose I am."

We both had a cold drink. Then I gave the shop boy a tip and got him to fetch Kamezo.

"I'm leaving things to you," I told him, "so just do whatever's necessary."

Kamezo went pale.

"You'll be in real trouble if you do this," he said. "I mean, it's stupid just when you're all set to make a name for yourself."

"D'you think I could call myself a yakuza if I couldn't stand up to some old businessman?"

"Yes, but still—what d'you aim to do?"

"The first thing is to talk it over with Okada."

So I went back to Tokyo, taking Omitsu with me. Then I left her at an inn and went to see Okada. After listening to what I had to say, he burst out:

"You just can't do that! There'll be a hell of a fuss if you aren't quick about it! The boss will throw a fit, for one thing. Look, it's still not too late—take the woman back where she came from!"

So I bowed to him and went back to the inn.

Looking back on it now, I really think I'd gone a bit funny in the head. I mean, to cut in on another man's woman, go against a warning from a senior member of the gang, and then make a run for it—I *must* have been crazy. But the one thing I knew was that I didn't want to break up with her, and I was quite prepared to be chucked out of the Dewaya.

I took Omitsu and we got on a train and went off into the country, to Saitama prefecture. After that we drifted from place to place—so many places it would take too long to tell you all the names. At Yudanaka hot springs, though, we stayed for about two weeks; it was the one place where we really took it easy, and it felt like we were really man and wife. But the sight of those hills every day somehow made me restless.

"I could get a job here as a maid in a hotel," Omitsu said to me eventually.

"Right, that's it, we're off!" I said, flying off the handle;

and we hit the road again.

It was tough going, but the girl never complained. Whenever I ran out of cash, I'd go and pay my respects to the local yakuza boss, hoping to get a bit of spending money. Quite a few of them, though, wouldn't have anything to do with me. It couldn't be helped—after all, they didn't have any obligations or anything to our gang.

I never took the girl with me on these visits; I'd leave her at a noodle restaurant or some other cheap eating place nearby and go on alone. They wouldn't let you near them if you went after sunset, either, so it had to be before it got dark. That was the rule.

At the entrance you gave the formal yakuza greeting. People in gangster films always seem to have it down pat, but it's not as easy as all that. It's like the way the samurai in the old days used to introduce themselves—you make it quite clear who you are, and what outfit you belong to, and who's your boss. These basic facts, and the way you deliver them, give them a good idea of what kind of guy you are. Anyway, I'd pay my respects to the local boss, and get given an envelope with a bit of cash in it, which kept us going for a while.

A formal greeting, yakuza-style

We'd left in August, and we wandered on in that way for more than three months. It might sound romantic, being together like that with someone you're in love with, but actually it's tough to be on the run all the time. On rainy days, for instance, it was awful. Country roads back then were hell to walk along. The whole road would be more like a paddy field—or a river, if the rain was heavy—with the mud splashing right up to your ass. If you had tall clogs on, the mud got stuck between the cleats and dragged down on your feet. You just *can't* go on walking forever in the rain, all wet through, sharing an umbrella with your woman, as they do in the movies. Like it or not, you take shelter in some room on the second floor of a cheap inn, and sit around doing nothing all day.

And however crazy you are about each other, you can't stay in bed screwing all the time, either; you don't feel like it, if you're tired and worried. Sometimes we'd be completely broke and have to sneak into a village shrine to spend the night, with only a single straw mat for bedding. We didn't know the area, so I'd get hold of a local and say to him, "My old man's been sick for months, and I'm traveling about praying for him. Are there any shrines around here that are known for answering people's prayers?" I didn't look the part, I'm sure, but he'd usually come up with some suggestion.

Not that that kind of place was ever comfortable to bed down in. It was toward the end of summer, you see, and there were swarms of mosquitoes. They bit right through our clothes. Normally, you'd light up a mosquito coil or something, but we couldn't allow smoke to be seen in a shrine—a wooden one, at that—as we might have been found by the villagers and reported to the police. So, however badly we got bitten, we just had to grin and bear it.

When we got too hungry to stand it any longer, I'd some-times steal things. I'd pinch a watermelon, or some sweet corn, which we gnawed at raw because there was nowhere to roast it.

Funnily enough, we didn't get sick. As for washing, they'd let us use the well if we asked at one of the farmer's houses. They'd lend us a bowl, too, so we could wash our underwear, then hang it on a pole and wait in just our kimonos till it dried. In the old days there was nothing unusual about peo-ple traveling around on foot, and the farmers were always helpful, giving them a cup of tea, letting them use their wells, and so on.

Even so, however tough you are, to go on walking every day without anywhere really to go wears you down in the end, physically and mentally. Travel's "sad and sore," as they used to say; sooner or later, you're bound to crack up.

It began to hurt just to look at Omitsu; the girl that used to work in Byodoken was gone completely. I got to feeling sad, thinking about all the fun she'd be having—wearing nice clothes, going to the theater and the movies—if only she hadn't fallen for me. So one day—we were walking along the edge of the Sano river at the time—I told her:

"I want you to go back to your parents' place, by yourself. I'll sort things out somehow on my own side."

"I'd rather kill myself than go home," she said, just like that. It was November by then, and the wind had a bite to it. She cried, and I got irritable. I made up my mind that the next day I really would leave her, and that night we went into the woods on some hills nearby and slept there, with her lying in my arms....

The next morning, the cold woke me up just as the sun

was rising. I looked around, and the girl had gone: nothing anywhere but bare trees. If people's hearts can really turn cold, as they say, that was just how I felt right then.

The idea that she'd run out on me gave me a queer feeling, part annoyed and part sorry for myself. I'd meant us to separate at any rate, but to have her go off of her own accord made me angry: people are funny like that. I pulled myself together and hunted around for her. No sign. Then, just as I was sitting on a stone in front of a little wayside shrine, I saw her in the distance, walking fast along a path between the paddy fields.

"Where the hell have you been?" I asked, but all the fire had gone out of me by then.

"I went and got some riceballs," she replied.

With Omitsu, on the run

She opened a package wrapped in bamboo leaves, and there were four riceballs inside. I was surprised that somebody'd been good enough to give them to her, but it turned out she'd given the ivory toggle on her sash for them. That made me do some hard thinking as I was eating my share: it's no good, I thought, we can't go on like this. So I said to her, "I can't stand seeing you like this any more. Before long I'll be a proper yakuza, and then I'll come and marry you, I promise. So you go back home for the time being." She cried, but in the end it was decided she should go.

I went with her as far as Koiwa, then went on alone to Funabashi, found an eating place where they knew me, and asked them to lend me a kitchen knife.

"Haven't seen you for ages, Eiji," said a cook with a cotton towel bound neatly around his forehead. "What do you want it for?"

"I'm going to use it here, so don't worry. I'll give it back to you right away."

He gave me the knife. I held one end of a bit of string I'd brought with me between my teeth, got hold of the other end with my right hand, and tied it around the little finger of my left hand. I pulled it as tight as I could. Then I chopped off the tip of the finger. The cook just stood there gawping, but it hurt too much for me to bother about him. I cut off one end of the clean white cotton of my bellyband, bound up the finger, then asked him for a sheet of paper. I wrapped the bit of finger in it, and left. I wasn't at all sure that cutting off a finger would be enough to make them let me off, but there wasn't any other way by now. So I set out for Makuta's place in a sort of what-the-hell mood.

When I called out in the entrance, a maid came out, and a young man with her. I introduced myself and said I'd come to apologize, and held out the finger, still wrapped in its piece of paper.

"Just wait there a second, will you?" the man said, and disappeared inside the house. I didn't know whether Makuta was in or not, but I could hear women talking at the back of the house. My hand by now was throbbing like hell, and my kimono was soaked with clammy sweat.

After a while the same man came out again and said, more politely than I'd expected,

"The boss says he understands. Now will you please leave?"

"I see," I said. "I'm much obliged." And I bowed and left.

It all went off so simply that I felt kind of let down. After that, I went straight back to Asakusa. On the way, I kept wondering why he'd made so little fuss, but I couldn't make any sense of it. So I assumed my boss must have done the apologizing for me. The boss was back in town by then. He glanced at me when I showed up, and said, "Mind you take yourself a bit more seriously from now on." And that was all he ever said about it.

I got a good talking-to from Okada, but Muramatsu wasn't even particularly angry. I remember him saying, "You're quite a character, aren't you?" Then he noticed me trying not to show the pain, and was decent enough to put me onto a good doctor; he even wrote a note to the surgery at the Yoshiwara hospital.

Incidentally, I didn't meet the girl again for years after that. I knew too well what would happen if I did, you see. A man's no match for a girl crying. I heard rumors that she left home soon after, but I was in Maebashi jail around then, so I wouldn't have been there even if she had come to Asakusa to see me.

147

III

I'd finished seeing my patients and was relaxing one Saturday after-noon when Hatsuyo dropped by.

"I wasn't sure about coming on a weekend like this," she told me, "but he said, the doctor always comes in the evening—it might be nice for once to give him a cup of tea while it's still light. And he asked me to pop along and ask you."

"How's his temperature?"

"Normal. He's gradually eating a bit more too. I was worried, I thought he'd never pull round this time, but he's stronger than you think, isn't he?"

Going into his living room, I noticed a flat dish lying on the low table. There was no water in it, but right in the center lay a large, lumpy black rock. The man had on a brown kimono of the kind they wear for tea ceremonies, tied with a black sash with a figured pattern.

"What's this?" I asked.

"It's a rock they use in what they call 'tray landscapes.' "

I peered more closely at the black rock in its dish.

"Mind if I pick it up?" I said.

"Go ahead."

It must have been a kind of lava. It was made up of a number of tight layers, with dark cracks in it here and there.

"There's grass growing on it, isn't there?"

"That's because it's a living thing. It was fifty years ago when I was given this. I was always making a mess of things in those days, and the boss was pretty disgusted with me, but one day he sent for me and said, 'Here, Eiji, I want you to look after this.' My mouth fell open. 'What is it, boss?' I asked. 'What am I supposed to do with a

lump of rock like this?' 'You give it water every morning and evening,' he said. I was a bit puzzled, but it was the boss's orders, so I took it back to my own room. And I gave it some water twice a day, but after a while I forgot to do it, and the next thing I knew it had gone. I forgot all about it for thirty or forty years, then all of a sudden it turned up again."

"Recently?"

"Eight years or so ago. It was with Kamezo, my junior. Kamezo died of lung cancer, but a month or so before he went he asked me over and said, 'Do you remember this?' 'Where on earth did you get it?' I asked, in surprise. 'When you were doing time in Maebashi I thought it would disappear if it was left where it was, so I put it away in a trunk, then forgot all about it. But as my wife was tidying up my things it turned up again. I thought that if I didn't give it back to you in a hurry it would get lost somewhere again, which is why I got you to come here.'

"Kamezo was a good, warmhearted friend, I never thought he'd go before me.... Anyway, I was grateful to him for keeping it for me like that. Now I'm old myself, I sort of understand what the boss felt about it, and I make a point of giving it some water once a day at least."

With a blanket over his bad leg and his arms folded lightly in his lap, he sat there gazing steadily at the rock.

The Bone-Sticker

I was twenty-six when they sent me to jail in Maebashi. I'd killed someone, you see, and I was in for over four years.

He was sitting with his feet in the sunken hearth, leaning against a back rest; he had a padded jacket over his kimono, and a muffler around his neck. The telephone lines were moaning in the wind above the roof.

Just north of the Ryounkaku in Asakusa, the twelve-story building like a pagoda that collapsed in the Great Earthquake, there used to be what they called "Gourd Pond." The district near it was packed with brothels, and I'd been put in charge of a gambling place right there among them.

It was a boiling hot day at the height of summer, I remember. Around noon, Muramatsu sent for me and asked if I'd mind taking someone in for a while.

"What kind of guy is he?" I said.

"You know Tomi in Shinagawa, don't you? He's a brother who helped me out once. Well, this fellow's the bookie at Tomi's place, a guy called Kiyomasa. Seems he's a good man, but from what I heard he caused some kind of trouble that put him on bad terms with the younger men. So they asked if we couldn't take him in here in Asakusa till they get it out of their system."

"I see."

"Just keep him out of the boss's way—you know how it is with him now."

Muramatsu was my senior as well, so of course I agreed to do it. I could see its advantages, in fact. A good bookie makes all the difference in a gambling joint—it's up to him whether a session comes alive or falls flat. At my own place, which was fairly small, Kamezo was the bookie, but with the best will in the world you could never have called him good at it.

When I actually met the guy, though, I had a feeling that something nasty was going to happen. The minute I saw his face, I felt we weren't going to hit it off. The feeling was right, too: I was going to end up killing him. It makes you think, doesn't it?... But it's too easy to make the facts fit after the event.

Anyway, I realized right off that with Kiyomasa around the gang could come unstuck. It was no good pretending to be senior in rank, in front of the younger men, if I was going to lose control over my place. I'd be ashamed in front of the boss, too. So I knew I'd have to do *something*; not bump him off, obviously—you don't kill a man just for that—but get him out of the way as soon as I could. But even kicking him out wasn't as easy as that, not with someone who'd been sent to Muramatsu by one of his brothers. So I decided to wait a while and see how it worked out.

In the end, it was about two months later that anything actually happened, but the seeds of trouble were there right from the start. There's a saying, "hate a priest, hate his cassock," and it's true: I took a dislike to every single thing about him. I expect it was the same with him as well.

On the outside at least, Kiyomasa was a good-looking guy, tall and with good features, straight nose, thick eyebrows, and a kind of brisk, convincing manner. And yet ...

"I hope I'll be satisfactory," he said to me when he first came, bowing his head as a junior should, but as he raised it again he flicked his eyes up at me as though to say, "You think I'll take orders from a kid like you?"

I was still only just over twenty-five at the time, and Kiyomasa was a good seven or eight years older, so I suppose it hurt his pride. But age doesn't matter in that business. As I said before, there are some men who are like the paneling in the john, however old they get, and there are others who become the main pillar of the house while they're still young. Age by itself just doesn't carry any weight.

That doesn't mean, though, that he was a dead loss, that he was no use to anybody; it wasn't as straightforward as that, which made it all the more awkward. To be fair, he had a real talent for organizing games, as you might expect in someone with such a punchy character.

When I first tried him out as our bookie, the way he called the betting and kept a general eye on things was all you could ask for. The games went like wildfire. He had a deep, husky voice and a good line in come-ons. The players lapped it up, and the bets came fast and furious. He made it exciting— made you feel you could almost *see* the spots on the dice in the cup.

Kiyomasa started getting popular, and the younger guys at our place were all behind him. The feeling was that he looked after them well, and for a while everybody got on fine. But it wasn't long before he began to show his own spots.

He was good, no doubt about it, but he was too proud of it—that was obvious too. He'd never actually say anything, but his expression had something snide about it. You could tell he didn't give a damn about you. I don't know why he always looked like that. That being his nature, I suppose, he couldn't stop it showing in his face. He'd do something to amuse the customers, then the next minute he'd give this nasty little smile. It's fatal in a professional gambler.

Let me tell you what happened one day. It was an evening

when there weren't many customers, and he said to me:

"There's not much action here, so how about it—why don't we play some *chiipa*?"

"It's an idea," I said. "But not tonight, there aren't enough of us. Let's leave it to some other time."

"When exactly is 'some other time'?" he asked with a little sneer.

This made me tense up, but I just told him not to worry, we'd do it soon, and that was the end of it for the time being. Even so, I couldn't help feeling it wasn't very bright of him—I mean, to say that kind of thing openly, in front of the customers. He was testing me, and, particularly with us yakuza, if somebody suggests in front of other people that you're not up to doing something, you're almost obliged to have it out with him. But maybe I'd better explain this all a bit more.

Just occasionally, if only a few customers show up, the professionals will have a game themselves, and one of the games they play is *chiipa*. When this happens, the ordinary players are asked to move away from the action and have to be satisfied with watching. In fact, once in a while, they'll hold a session specially to play *chiipa*, with nobody but yakuza in the room. Though I doubt whether any yakuza nowadays know the proper way to play it....

In ordinary games, you have two dice and gamble on the odds or evens, but in *chiipa* you have four. All different sizes, too. The biggest of them is called *daito*. The second, which is yellow, is *nishuku*. The third has its eyes painted red, so it's called *akappa*. And the smallest of the lot is *chibiri*. All different, both in size and color. The players stake their money on one particular dice or the other, in various combinations.

Everybody present is a professional, so you don't have to

work up an atmosphere. The bookie, for example, never calls out "Place your bets, then, place your bets." Nobody talks at all, in fact. And the stakes are higher than usual, too. The people around you are all professional gamblers, so there's a different look in their eyes. About the only thing you can hear is the sound of money being put down and the rustling of kimonos.

A dice game

After a while, when he thinks the time is right, the bookie says, "That's all, gentlemen," and everybody has to take their hands away from the cash. Once they've done that, he says "Play," in a quiet voice. And that's when the money moves.

Anyhow, that was the game Kiyomasa suggested we should play. But you see, the guy knew perfectly well that it wasn't possible at my place. Serious gambling never goes right unless you've got the right people. To play *chiipa*, you've got to have solid bosses or professional gamblers who come regularly to your place.

"Listen, Eiji," Kamezo said to me later. "Are you going to let him get away with that? He's getting above himself, the bastard."

"Never mind," I told him. "He just said what he felt without thinking. In fact, why don't we do as he says sometime soon?"

Actually, though, I'm not as cool or forgiving as I might have sounded. I was furious, and tucked the incident away at the back of my mind.

With things as they were, I was just thinking of telling Muramatsu that I couldn't take responsibility for this man any more, when there was a bit of trouble, and over a very minor thing at that. One evening, Kiyomasa got drunk and pissed on a brothel signboard. It was late at night, and I suppose he thought there wasn't anybody looking. Actually, the place was shut, and they didn't realize what was going on. But a woman in the vegetable shop on the other side of the road saw him at it. Even so, if it had happened only once there wouldn't have been any fuss, I suppose, but it seemed Kiyomasa was always pissing on signs in the area whenever he got a bit drunk. Word of it got around, and one day, when one of the lower-ranking members of our outfit—"Little Mitsu," we all called him—was going by, the woman stopped him and complained.

"Here, you—" she said, "there's one of your people goes about every night peeing on the signs around here. The sort of thing even a dog would be ashamed to do. If your boss goes on letting him get away with it, it's going to ruin his reputation."

Little Mitsu was a bit shaken by this, and the least he could do was ask her to lend him a bucket so he could get some water from the well and wash the signs down. He went around to the other establishments near there, apologizing to the owners, then came to tell me what had happened.

"I see...," I said. "I was already thinking of talking to Muramatsu about him myself. So hang on till I can do something about it."

But Mitsu was too upset to be calmed down as easily as all that. He went and found Kiyomasa and complained to him directly:

"Look, Kiyo—I know you were drunk, but if you go around doing that kind of thing, it's going to hurt Eiji's reputation, right?"

Now, any normal member of the gang would just have apologized and that would have been the end of it, but Kiyomasa wasn't like that. He just flared up, and since there wasn't much he could say as an excuse, he shouted something about Mitsu teaming up with the woman to spy on him.

This got Little Mitsu going too, of course.

"OK, you shithead," he yelled back at him. "You think you can pull rank on me? *Nobody* talks to me like that."

So Kiyomasa ups and belts him in the face. Mitsu then lets him have it, saying he'll kill him.

Luckily, that time, Kamezo went in and separated them, and Kiyomasa came to me later and apologized, down on his knees. Which settled things for the moment. But Kamezo kept on telling me to get rid of him, and the others felt the same way too. So I thought: well, *that* should be enough to convince Muramatsu, and I made up my mind to go and see him, the next day if possible.

Before I could get around to it, though—that very same day, in fact—there was another row. I wasn't there when it started, but from what I heard later Kiyomasa suddenly picked on Little Mitsu and insisted he take him to see the woman who said she'd seen him pissing. When Mitsu asked what he meant to do, he just glared at him and told him to mind his own business—shut up and take me to her, he said.

159

That made Mitsu really start slanging him. And *that* made Kiyomasa come in fighting. The other guys there tried to hold him back, but he was too strong for them. So Kamezo ran out to get me.

As for what happened next—well, I'll just stick to the main points, as it got really messy. Kiyomasa must have gone completely off his rocker. He rushed out into the kitchen, grabbed hold of a gimlet, and set on Mitsu with it. (It was a three-pronged thing we'd got to break up the ice for the little pillows we used when we took a nap in summer.) Then, when I waded in to try and stop him, he suddenly turned on me instead.

"I'm going to kill you!" he shouted, coming for me, so I picked up a kitchen knife that was lying around—the "bone-sticker," we used to call it, a kind of stiletto—and stuck him in the chest. It went clean through a rib and into his heart. The blood spurted out, and I got splashed red all over.

It was a dancing teacher, who happened to turn up just then, who called the police. A whole crowd of them came rushing over. They took in what had happened, and an elderly detective asked me:

"Eiji, was it you that did it?"

"Yes, it was me," I said.

They all knew me well enough, so they didn't use the handcuffs.

I was sent from the police lockup to Ichigaya. And then there was the trial. It was only then that it really came home to me just what a big man the Dewaya boss was. Nobody else could have done what he did: running all over the place, getting up a petition to present in court, and so on.

He and Muramatsu covered everywhere they could think

of in Asakusa—all the shops along the approach to the temple, for example—getting hundreds of people to sign. When a detective told me about him going around from shop to shop—and he was sick, you know—bowing his head to people for their signatures, it brought the tears to my eyes. I actually put my hands together, there in the lockup, and said a little prayer of thanks to him.

And it wasn't just signatures, either. He actually went to Kiyomasa's parents and got them to put in a plea for manslaughter, not murder.

It seems Kiyomasa was the son of a timber wholesaler. But he got mixed up with a gang of young hoods, and one thing led to another till he was stealing his parents' money, getting women into trouble, and generally getting so out of hand that his father asked the boss in Shinagawa to take him over.

The father must have given him up as a bad job, because when he wrote to the court he said he'd been half resigned to something like that happening. It was a miracle, in fact, that Kiyomasa had lived as long as he had, he said. In a way, he'd brought it on himself, making a nuisance of himself at the first place he was taken in, and ending up pulling a knife on someone. His father didn't bear me any grudge, and his other children didn't either, so they hoped they wouldn't charge me with too serious a crime....

The boss even got a politician in on it, too, a man called Okubo, who had a lot of support in Asakusa. This Okubo, apparently, introduced him to a lawyer and did all kinds of other things to help as well.

It took a year before they reached a verdict. I wasn't charged with murder, but with inflicting bodily injury resulting in death, and I got five years. So, after keeping me in Sugamo for a while, they sent me on to Maebashi with a handful of other prisoners—by train, in a coach we had to ourselves. I'd been in detention for a year already, which left four years to do in Maebashi.

The Jellywobbles

"*I don't suppose you know what it's like inside a jail, do you, doctor?*"

"*I know a bit about it.*"

"*Really? How's that, then?*"

"*Sometimes, if a prisoner gets hurt or sick, I get called in to see him.*"

"*And how about it—I mean, your impression of what you've seen inside?*"

"*It's interesting, in its way. They can be pretty tricky.*"

"*Pretending to be sick?*"

"*Yes. Most of the time, of course, they really are sick, but there are some of them who try to fake it. They're quite good at it, too. Groaning with pain, even making themselves break out in a sweat—if you're not careful, you can fall for it.*"

The man chuckled. "*I'm not surprised,*" he said; "*some of those guys are pretty sharp. A young doctor could easily get had. But there are all kinds of doctors too, you know. The Maebashi jail where I was had its own medic, and he was a real bastard. He'd never come straightaway, even if the prisoner was in real pain. Absolutely refused to get up if it was at night. He'd write the death certificates himself, but most other things he left to the warders. We didn't dare get sick because of what might happen.*"

The thing about Maebashi was the cold. Looking back on it now, I get the feeling it was always winter there. The jail was by the river Tone, on the edge of the town, and you could hear the water roaring past; it got on your nerves at night, when an empty belly kept you awake. Way up in the north there were the Akagi mountains, and a cold wind blew down off them. There was an eighteen-foot-high wall around the place, and the wind went round and round inside it. The sound of it alone was enough to make you feel cold.

At the Sugamo jail there were twelve men to a cell, but in Maebashi there was only six. At night, you slept on one thin quilt spread on the tatami; it was terribly small—not three feet wide, more like two foot eight or nine, I'd say. And about five foot six long. I'm tall, so my legs stuck out at the end. The top quilts were a bit bigger all around. But they'd all been in use for years, and they were so old there was hardly any cotton stuffing left in them. Actually, it was still there, but the quilt had been reserviced so many times it had gone flat and hard. It wasn't an even thickness, either—there were lumps in places, like islands in the sea; where the islands were, the quilt bulged, but the other places were so flat they were mostly cloth and nothing else. Not much chance of a good night's rest when even your top quilt was like that....

The warders put me to work making paper bags. There were other men doing the same job; fifteen of them were yakuza. They say a yakuza in jail is like a nightsoil dipper that's lost its handle—the shit's still there, but no way you can use it. A bad joke, but it's not far off the mark.

The yakuza never do any proper work in ordinary life, so it's no wonder they can't do any when they're put inside. I mean, you could hardly tell them to organize gambling sessions, could you? But you can't leave them idle, either, so they get taught some simple job or other. Sticking bags together is just the thing for yakuza, as it's only simple repetition.

There was a boss from Kiryu called Kanjiro in with me—Kan-chan, people called him. I soon got friendly with him, and we kept it up for years even after we were outside again. And there was another one too, who went by the name of Muraoka Kenji. With him, I struck up a brother relationship.

This Muraoka was closely connected with the Kodama organization, which, years later, got mixed up in the Lockheed scandal. He came in a while after me. Then there were two others, Tsunegoro and Namiji, who became sort of recruits of mine and helped me in all kinds of ways.

I never did find out just what Muraoka was in for, but Kanchan was in because he was framed by the police.

"It was diabolical, what they did," said Kan-chan as he stood next to me, pasting bags. "This dick turns up at my place and tells me to hand over a couple of pistols. Now, I ask you—have *you* ever had guns around? No? Of course you haven't. After all, I hear you used a bone-sticker for the job that got you in this time. Smart, I call it."

"What's so smart about it?"

"No need to be modest, now.... Anyway, that was what this copper said to me, so I dug my heels in and said I didn't have any. But he wasn't having any of that. Well then, he says, you'll have to go out and *buy* some, and then turn them in. In the end, he started threatening me—said if I didn't come up with them he'd have my place raided. That really pissed me off. Go on then, do it, I said. And—sure enough, like good honest cops—raid us they did, the bastards, that same night. Right in the middle of a session. Caught red-handed. And here I am."

Kan-chan seemed really burned up about it. The real reason why the police set him up, of course, was to improve the district's anti-crime record. Sometime after I left jail—around 1938, I suppose it would have been—I had just the same kind of trouble myself at my joint in Uguisudani. Told me, in just the same way, to hand in my guns. This particular detective came straight from the Metropolitan Police Board—the very top. I expect they'd been tipped off that some yakuza somewhere had got hold of a few pistols, so they planned to make a clean sweep. But there weren't any in my place to begin with, and there was nothing I could do.

So they told me to produce some even if I had to buy them. It was way out of line, but if I'd gone on insisting I didn't have any, I'd have ended up the same as Kan-chan, so I got a brother to buy me a couple at three hundred and fifty yen apiece. That was enough to buy a house with in those days, but I couldn't afford to think about that.

I turned them in to the police immediately. "Good work," they said—and that was the last I heard about it: no letter of thanks, and no punishment, either....

Anyway, with one thing and another, Kan-chan and I got on together like a house on fire, and we were always talking to each other in whispers in the workshop. We went too far, though—the warders got pissed off, and we ended up in trouble.

It was the day after there'd been a fall of snow. It was always twice as cold after snow. At night, it got steadily chillier and chillier, and people had to take a leak all the time. You'd just be dropping off to sleep, and somebody would make a clatter getting up. Then as soon as one man had finished, another would get up. This went on all through that night, but in the end I must have dozed off, because I suddenly woke up to hear a warder calling me.

"What d'you want at this time of night?" I asked.

"Come on out," he said, so I shambled out, only to find

myself handcuffed on the spot.

"What's this for?" I shouted. "I haven't done anything, have I?" So another warder swiped me across the face. It turned out that my crime was communicating with another prisoner—i.e, talking to Kan-chan behind the warders' backs. So I was hauled to my feet, marched along the corridor, and taken into a bare, concrete room. Kan-chan joined us on the way. In the middle of the room was a sort of small swimming pool. "Get in that," they told me. There was a single light hanging from the ceiling.

"Hurry up!" the warder kept shouting at me. I was hand-cuffed, so there wasn't anything I could do, but the night was already cold enough to make you shake, and a "swim" could easily have killed you. I glanced over in Kan-chan's direction; he was looking over at me, too. That gave them the chance to give me a shove, and I found myself underwater before I even had time to yell.

It wasn't as deep as all that, but the bottom was slippery, and it was hard to find your feet. Not being able to use my hands, I choked and swallowed a hell of a lot of water. Then the warder grabbed hold of my handcuffs and dragged my face up to the edge of the pool, so I managed to get some breath, but I was in a terrible state—I mean, I was past being just *cold*, I thought I was going to pass out.

"How about it?" the warder was saying above my head. "Are you going to do as we say?"

I was in no state to say anything, but I managed to get out a "Fuck you!" so he kicked me in the face and I went under again. The second time he hauled me up, I could hear him still saying "Are you going to do as we say?" I was past talking, though—I couldn't even breathe. They finally dragged me out, but my body was all stiff, it felt as if I was wearing armor.

The water was dripping in great drops from the bottom of my kimono. The funny thing is, I felt like I was hot, as though I'd been burned all over.

But when I got back to the cell and got in between the quilts, I started shivering and couldn't stop. It's a wonder you can be treated like that and not die. Kan-chan got a fever and couldn't get up for a week.

It was cold at other times too—like when we came back from work every day. That was when you saw what we used to call "the jellywobbles." Between the workshop and the cell-block, there was a changing room where the prisoners took off their work clothes and put their uniforms back on. The windows there were always wide open, and the outside air came blowing straight in, so that we had to strip off in a freezing draft.

First they had a roll call, and as soon as your number was called you stripped off. Then you had to put your hands over your head and stand there with your legs apart, while the warder circled you to make sure you didn't have anything on you. When he'd finished checking, you put your prison uniform on. That was the roughest part of it. I mean, the clothes had been left out all day on a shelf. And they were dirty, too; we were allowed to wash them from time to time, but only with water, no soap. So they were thick with years of sweat and grime, which froze into something like ice, so when that came in contact with your skin, you couldn't help starting to shiver. Your face, your jaws, your belly, your arms and legs—they all shook, there was no way of hiding it. People talk about it being so cold "you can't get your teeth together"—well, that just about describes it. Even if you wanted to say something, your jaw was shaking too much to get anything out.

It's a funny thing, that kind of trembling. It's not something you can stop by sheer effort. You try to control it so it won't show, but it's just impossible. Even the toughest fellow trembles. That was what the prisoners used to call "the jelly-wobbles."

In those days, prisons didn't have glass windows or anything like that. There were sliding doors with bars, pasted over with paper like shoji. When the paper got old it turned yellow and cracked so that drafts came blowing in. Maebashi had been built in 1888, if I remember rightly, and everything in it was worn out.... The cells and corridor, too, were separated by the same kind of sliding doors—I suppose it was a kind of hangover from the old-style, all-wooden jails of the past.

There were four other men in the same cell with me. The one who'd been there longest was an umbrella repairman called Toyama. There was also a man who sold matches, a handsome guy who thought he looked like Gary Cooper, but I've forgotten his name. Toyama the umbrella man had been put inside for murdering his wife after she ran off with someone else.

Almost everybody gets a kind of run-down look when they're in a prison cell, but Toyama looked particularly seedy. He had a round face, with a little nose sticking out of it like a nipple, and drooping eyes. He was a timid fellow, always kowtowing to the warders; I don't think it was just because he was in jail, I'm sure he'd been like that even when he was working outside.

Toyama and his wife had been living for years in a cheap tenement behind a horsemeat store, but in the year it happened there'd been a bad drought, with next to no business even in the so-called rainy season. Umbrella men don't get much work even at the best of times, so I reckon that when things got really bad they couldn't make a living at all. So they were helping at the store, going around buying up horse-meat.

It seems the guy who stole Toyama's wife was one of those men with a little stall on wheels who used to go around cleaning out the tiny pipes that people smoked tobacco in. When Toyama came home one day, after he'd been out buying up horses, his wife was out. Several days went by and still she didn't come home. He'd just about given her up for good when one day—it was raining for the first time in ages—he heard the pipe-cleaning man going by on a back street near the house, blowing that funny little horn they used to have. Toyama happened for once to be busy repairing an umbrella, but he had a kind of uneasy feeling, so he put his work down and went outside to look. Just outside the entrance there was a stream, with a narrow road running along the other side. And there was the pipe-cleaning man, hauling his stall along through the mud, blowing his horn as he went. And walking along behind the stall was a woman.

"If I'm not mistaken, I thought, that's my wife," he told me. "My wife, holding up a little umbrella in the pouring rain, traipsing along behind him.

"I rushed out of the house in a kind of frenzy. I soon caught up with them.

" 'You come with me!' I shouted, tugging at her.

" 'Hey, stop that!' the man said, but I knocked him down and went off dragging her along with me, across the stream at the back of the stables, and into a graveyard that stood by the stream.

"It was raining buckets, and the drops were bouncing off

the gravestones. I grabbed my wife by the scruff of the neck. 'What's all this about?' I asked her.

" 'I'm fed up with you,' she said. 'I'm leaving you.'

" 'Don't be a fool!' I said, grabbing the front of her kimono and almost pleading with her. 'We've been together ever since we were twenty!' That made her look as if she was going to cry, and she said, 'It's all over.' So I hit her.

"Then I asked, 'Is it really over?' and she just went on nodding her head—like a drowned rat, she looked—so I hit her again, hardly knowing what I was doing. I think I knocked her back over a gravestone. But however much I think about it, I can't remember what happened after that. The first thing I knew, she was dead, and for some reason or other I was standing there with an umbrella in my hand."

"Was it your wife's umbrella?"

"She was lying on the ground in front of a grave with a little statue of Jizo on it. There was a puddle by it that was bright red. I was holding the umbrella, but why I was holding it I've no idea. There was blood dripping from the tip of it, and it was that, running down the gravestone, that made the puddle."

He dreamed about his wife sometimes, Toyama said. The funny thing was, they were always pleasant dreams, and his wife was always in a good mood.

"I sometimes think, you know, that deep in her heart she was glad I killed her. I mean, would she ever have been any happier with the pipe-cleaning man than with me?"

Toyama had been sentenced to six years in prison; when I met him he was just starting on his fourth year.

I'd been in jail for about a year when the Dewaya boss died. He'd always had a bad chest, and we hadn't really expected him to live to a ripe old age, but it came as a terrible shock when I actually heard that he was dead. Something more than just feeling sad. Kan-chan from Kiryu was quite concerned about me. "Pull yourself together, now," he said. "It's not like you, this isn't." Yes, it really hit me hard.

It never rains but it pours, though, doesn't it? And only five or six days later, word came that the woman he lived with, the gang's "elder sister," had also died.

This time I could hardly believe it. The boss had already been sick, and I'd been half resigned to it, but she was only around thirty and quite healthy, and it didn't seem possible she'd died of illness. If it wasn't illness, then something must have happened, but I hadn't a clue what it could be. I kept fretting about it. After a while, though, Kamezo came to visit me, and he gave me all the details.

According to Kamezo, the cause of the boss's death had been morphine poisoning. "The doctor came every day and injected him with pain-killers, but the trouble in his lungs had spread all through his body, and he was in awful pain, it was terrible just to see him, and in the end she gave him enough morphine to put him out of his misery."

The boss must have realized that he didn't have much longer to live. He summoned Sekine—his chief brother boss —and the rest of the gang to his bedside. This Sekine was the man who started the Matsubakai, a big yakuza syndicate, and one of the most powerful men in the business. He and the boss of the Dewaya had been brothers of the same rank for years, and our boss must have felt there might be trouble afterward if he didn't bring Sekine in to help.

What he said to Sekine was this: "It seems I'm not long for this world," he said, "and there's something I want to talk to you about. When I die, I want you to keep an eye on Muramatsu here, as the next head of the Dewaya. I'd like you to help him in his career, as your younger brother—it can be a six-four relationship, say, or seven-three if that won't do."

In a way, this amounted to our boss's will, Sekine felt, so he said, "Right. I'll do my best on my own side too to keep up the Dewaya's good name. Muramatsu's a man of real ability, I'm sure he'll make a worthy successor. Anyway, you don't have to worry yourself—I'll look after him properly from now on."

This seems to have taken a load off the boss's mind. After that, apparently, he just stayed in bed all day long, waiting for the end. The pain got worse and worse. The disease had got right into his bones, so that when he moved they crumbled—it must have been agony. The injections the doctor gave weren't enough for him to put up with it, so he got the doctor to let him have some of the drug and had his woman inject it for him.

In those days, nobody made a fuss about morphine and the like, and you didn't have to be underhand about it like you do nowadays. It was only after Japan lost the war and the occupation forces came in that people began to get stuffy about drugs; before the war, you could get hold of them easily enough if you knew a doctor. That was how the boss, too, ended up becoming an addict.

One day, when he was gradually getting weaker and weaker, he had a talk with his woman:

"I'm grateful for all you've done for me," he said. "But you've got to plan for the future—you're still young, after all. Without me around to help, you'll find it tougher going than before. You've got to make your own decisions, and act responsibly so that you aren't a burden on the others."

Kamezo and two or three other men were by his bed at the

173

time. They'd all been wondering what he was going to say, but what they actually heard was so sad they started crying. How could anybody have thought of treating their "elder sister" badly just because the boss was dead?...

She liked sewing, and used to make all the boss's clothes herself. Most of the rest of us, too, must have had at least one or two things that she'd run up for us. She was that kind of woman, so she was popular, and if ever she was sharp with someone, they'd do as she said without a murmur. And yet in the end, once the boss's funeral was over, she went into her own room, bound her knees with a waistband, and killed herself with an injection of morphine in the thigh....

The bosses of the other gangs there at the funeral thought it was a bit funny she'd disappeared so suddenly, so Muramatsu told the others to go and look for her, otherwise we'd all lose face. And after hunting all over the place, they found her lying there. Naturally, there was a hell of a fuss. Some of the guests said, "Why did she have to kill herself, it wasn't as if she was General Nogi's wife?..." Others thought she must have felt to blame, seeing as she'd been injecting the boss with morphine three times a day. Anyway, it was a sad business, and for once I actually felt critical of the boss: what did you have to take her with you for, I felt like asking him.

But there I was, stuck away from it all in jail. So I made up my mind to serve my term properly and get released as soon as possible. I felt the boss wouldn't really rest in peace until I'd got out and been to put some flowers on his grave and burn some incense.

I worked really hard after that. The average prisoner would be lucky if he finished a hundred bags in a day, so *I* tried to do two hundred. I didn't do shoddy work, either: the bags were all exactly the right size, with no paste spreading outside the flaps, no dirty marks on the paper. I went on like that every day for a year and a half. It made the warders begin to look at me differently. And my ranking went up steadily. Before two years were up, I was at the top of the ladder.

In jail, they make a clear-cut distinction between the different convicts. There are five ranks. Men in the lowest rank are called "greenies"—maybe because they've only just got in and are still fairly fresh. From there you move up to fourth rank, third rank, and so on, and by the time you've reached the top, you're a "trustie." You start wearing different clothes, for one thing. Instead of the reddish prison uniform, you're allowed to wear what you like, within reasonable limits. You can buy yourself a sweater with the money you've earned pasting bags or envelopes. You can buy underwear. And you can have food sent in.

As soon as I'd reached the top grade, I bought some woolen undershirts and long johns. It was like going to heaven. You know—the first time a woman gets a fur coat and puts it on I'm sure she feels happy, but I doubt if it's anything compared with how I felt when I put on my woolies. For a start, I found I could sleep really tight at night. When I woke up in the morning, my tiredness was gone. That was a real blessing.

Why were we allowed these things? It was a reward system, that's all. Look, they'd say—if you do your best, *you* can be like that man too, so take a leaf out of his book and get to work. It meant, too, that even if you reached the top grade you soon got demoted again if you slackened off or broke the rules.

I was lucky, though—I didn't get demoted; in fact I went one notch above the first rank, where they gave you a good conduct badge. I ended up with two of them, the only man in the whole jail wearing two at once. And I became the foreman of the workshop.

What that meant in practice was that I acted as a sort of assistant warder. There were just two warders in charge of a great crowd of prisoners at work. One was the chief, the other his deputy. The chief sat high up in front of a desk where he could keep an eye on everything. The deputy spent all his time prowling around the workshop itself.

Apart from them, there'd be one or two instructors. These weren't officials, they were ordinary people who came to the prison every morning. And we were glad to have them. Besides teaching the men how to do the work, they brought in news from outside. Not just old news, either—they knew what had happened the day before, or the same day. According to the rules, they weren't supposed to have any conversation with the prisoners that wasn't to do with the work in hand. But they were human too, and they'd have been bored just talking shop. So they used to chat about this and that, in a quiet voice, almost like they were talking to themselves. And the cons would ask them questions, almost like *they* were talking to themselves as well. In that way, we got to hear all kinds of things. It wasn't that the deputy warder didn't realize what was going on, but so long as it didn't go too far he'd pretend not to notice.

Having been to a commercial school as a kid, I wasn't bad at figures and keeping accounts, and it was my job to help the chief warder keep up the records. I kept track of how much each prisoner had done, how well it had turned out, etc.—all entered in little notebooks for each man. It was quite a responsibility. I mean, it all depended on me whether a particular guy went down as doing a good job or not. It gave me a kind of authority. Of course, I saw to it that none of the other men suffered, but at the same time I made sure my own pals came out ahead.

I'll tell you how it worked. Every month there were almost always two or three men who finished their terms and left jail—sometimes as many as five or six. Most of them didn't go on the first of the month but on the tenth, or halfway through, and since they went on working to the end, that meant that what they'd already produced was left over. Where they were going, of course, the records in their little books wouldn't mean a thing any more, so the stuff was up for grabs until the end of the month, when everything was handed over to whoever ran the business. So I'd add it on to the work done by my pals. It would have been too much to give all the credit to any one man, so I'd divide it up among them, a little each. It was all up to me.

The warders knew what I was doing. But they didn't say anything, even so. In a prison, you see, it pays to give the best prisoners a certain power. That way, I added on quite a lot for Kan-chan from Kiryu, and for Muraoka, who came in later. And I did the same for men like Tsunegoro and Namiji, who were sort of on my team. You'd be surprised at the effect it had. I mean, a man was naturally pleased to see twelve hundred envelopes written down in his book when he knew he'd only made nine hundred that month. There'd have been a fuss, of course, if you did somebody else out of work he'd done and tacked it on to a friend's, but that never happened. Besides, prisoners only got to see their own personal records, so nobody had any idea whether other people were doing better or not; so long as the number of envelopes they'd made and the figure in the book matched, there was nothing for them to complain about.

Anyway, I used to look after my friends in ways like that; but I helped out the warders too, in a different kind of way, by acting as a lookout for them. The warders were supposed to keep an eye on the prisoners' movements at all times, but they were only human, and occasionally they'd feel like taking a nap. Or if they'd got a lot of paperwork on hand, they'd naturally want to get it done while they were on duty. So when I could see that a warder wanted to be doing something different, I'd say, "Here—you get on with it, I'll stand in for you."

Then I'd tip off Tsunegoro or Namiji or somebody in advance—tell them that if the prison governor was coming they were to let me know before he opened the door. They were sharp lads, and only too happy to do as I said. So when the governor came along the corridor, one of the guys keeping an eye open as he worked would give me a signal.

"The boss's coming, chief," I'd whisper. And the chief warder would shut his ledger, get up from his chair, and start looking around the workshop.

"Well? Everything OK?" the governor would ask when he arrived.

And the chief warder would give a salute and reply,

"Everything normal, sir!"

That was how things went, and, not surprisingly, I was the warders' pride and joy.

Captain Hashiba

It must have been May 1936 when I was released. I was thirty-one by then, and it was just the time of the Abe Sada incident; I remember seeing the headlines in the papers.

It made a terrific stir at the time—I mean, a restaurant manager's mistress killing him and chopping off his pecker, then walking around with it in her purse—and when I came out of jail the men waiting to meet me at the gates—Muraoka and Kan-chan, and members of my outfit—they couldn't talk about anything else.

"You'd better look out from now on, Eiji," said Kamezo. "With things as they are these days, next time you make a fool of yourself with a woman you won't get away with losing just your little finger. No amount of guts is going to help you if you get yourself chopped like that!"

"Forget it," I said. "This is my first whiff of the outside world in four years. I don't care whether it's Abe Sada or who it is—any woman'll do, so you just go and get me half a dozen!"

I made a joke of it at the time, but the best thing of all out there in the streets *was* the women; whenever one went by in a kimono and with her hair all done up, I couldn't help staring. I'd never realized there were so many pretty women around.

So when I arrived at Ueno station I was in a really good mood for the first time in ages. I changed trains and went on to Kuramae, and was just getting into a rickshaw when I saw some soldiers with rifles on their shoulders tramping past on the other side of the road. As I watched, another platoon shouldering rifles came along.

"Letting us see them marching all over the town, eh?" I said. "They must need something to do."

"I expect they're going off for training somewhere," Shiro said. "Because of the incident."

"What incident?"

"You mean you don't know?" he said, giving me a doubtful look.

There'd been an army rebellion that February, he told me. A bunch of young officers had tried to take control, and Tokyo had been put under martial law; there'd been quite a flap, apparently. I looked interested and surprised, though shocked was what I really felt.

It was the February 26 Incident, of course. In jail, we'd got wind of most things that were happening, but this time I hadn't heard a thing; neither the warders nor the instructors had told us about it. It made me feel after all that those eighteen-foot walls weren't there for nothing.

When I got back to the Dewaya, I paid my respects to Muramatsu, then went straight on to visit the boss's grave. You know, the gravemarker was already looking a bit weather-beaten. It brought home to me how long I'd been away. I just stood there staring at the boss's Buddhist name written on the marker, and couldn't say anything for a while.

As soon as I was back from the cemetery, Muramatsu said he had something to talk about and took me into the back room.

"You've probably heard already," he said, "but Shunkichi's left town."

He was right, I already knew about it, but now I heard the details. There'd been a police raid while they were all hard at it gambling, and Shunkichi—who ran the joint—had skipped out and never come back.

"That was the fourth time they'd been raided," Muramatsu said, folding his arms and frowning. "It makes you sick."

"So where is he now, then?"

"I don't know myself. The bastard!"

Shunkichi was no coward, so it probably wasn't the police that had made him run. He'd never been on the best of terms with Muramatsu, and things had got worse after the boss died. I was only guessing, but that seemed a more likely reason.

"I'm not going to go looking for him," said Muramatsu. "So I'm thinking of letting you have his place. How about it?"

"If you want me to, I'll take it on," I said. "But is it OK with Shunkichi's guys?"

"That depends on how you handle them," he said.

I was prepared for this—I'd had an idea it might happen even while I was still inside—so I thanked him and agreed. And that's how I got my own gambling joint in Uguisudani.

"Are you familiar with Uguisudani, doctor?" the man asked.

"I've been there to visit the Kishimojin shrine," I said.

"Oh yes?... They hold a morning-glory fair there nowadays, don't they—selling the flowers in little pots."

"Yes, I went last year. There was quite a turnout."

"I rather like it myself. My joint wasn't in that district, though, but over by the river. There used to be old mansions with big gardens and plum trees in the area, where people would bring their pet nightingales to have singing competitions with each other. There weren't many left by my time, though."

"How about the gambling place—is there anything of that left nowadays?"

"Not a trace of it. The whole area was burned down in the air

181

raids, and the river was covered in later, so now there's nothing but
shops. Even I have a hard job finding my way around. A real shame
it's all gone...."

In getting my gambling place going, Muramatsu helped
with the funds, and Kan-chan and Muraoka both helped as
well, so somehow or other I managed to get it on its feet in
fairly good time. I also managed to get married.

Her name was Omon. She was a geisha in Asakusa; we'd
become lovers a while before, and ended up living together.
I'd had quite a bit of trouble, though, getting to that stage.

What happened was that her dancing teacher and her
mother ganged up together to keep her out of my clutches.
The mother, Tsuru, was an ex-geisha too, and she'd brought
Omon up all by herself, and as she was obviously fond of her
daughter she wanted to find her a good patron if she could
—and live a comfortable life herself on the strength of it. That
was *her* idea, and I suppose it was only natural, because Omon
was popular as a geisha, and there'd been any number of
men who wanted to make her their mistress. The thing was,
though, that Omon said it was *me* she wanted to marry.

That sent Tsuru right up the wall. There were endless
quarrels between them, and the mother came in tears to see
me and beg me to give her up. Tears or not, though, that was
too much to ask; I might have done it if Omon herself had
said she wanted to split up, but she didn't, so there wasn't
anything I could do. Anyway, after a lot of wrangling, Tsuru
gave in, looking fit to howl.

That made *me* feel pretty bad about it, too, so I went to see
her several times to try and bring her around. But she still
hadn't really given up the fight. Whenever I went, she had
some complaint or other to make. The bitching just went on

182

and on. If I kept quiet—she *was* the girl's mother, after all —she just took advantage of it, got carried away.

In the end, I decided things couldn't go on like that, there was no telling what would happen. So one day I stuck a knife in my sash and took Kamezo, with a coil of rope around his shoulder, and burst in on the dancing master and Tsuru just as they were having a nice cup of tea together. We looked pretty threatening, and it shook them up.

"What do you want?" they said, and tried to get away, but their legs just buckled under them. So we grabbed hold of them, bound them up, side by side, with the rope, then flung the end over a beam and hauled them up in the air. Then I drove the knife home into the tatami underneath them.

"Well—how about it?" I said. "D'you want to go on as you've been doing? Or will you stop complaining about us from now on?" They just hung there, too startled to say anything. So this time Kamezo said:

"See here, lady. Eiji's a big man in our business. I mean, you'll be much better off with him than if you'd made the girl some rich man's mistress. Look—he's offering to fix you up for the rest of your life, so why not relax and enjoy life together?"

Tsuru by now had gone quite pale and just nodded and grunted, again and again. So we pulled the knife out of the floor and let them down.

"Well, then," I said, putting my hands in front of me on the tatami and bowing down low. "I'm sorry things got a bit rough. But that's the way I am, and I just hope we can get on better for a long time to come." And before I left I put an envelope with some money in it on the table.

She never made any more fuss, you know. I'd drop in occasionally to leave some pocket money for her, and she'd just sit there, all quiet and shrunk up. I was hoping she might call it quits and cheer up, but it wasn't to be. So I left her to it, and Omon herself didn't say anything more about her, either.

Without either of us wanting it particularly, we soon had another woman on our hands. It happened like this.

It was the end of 1937, when business was good at my place and I was getting to be a proper boss in the gambling world. One day, I had an early bath, then put on a kimono and went out for a stroll in Asakusa with Kamezo. We were walking along when I saw this Salvation Army man in an old-fashioned uniform standing at the corner of a little shopping street, beating a drum and asking for money. Even nowadays you still see them sometimes in the better parts of town, but in the old days the Salvation Army was very active everywhere, preaching and fund-collecting at the same time. So I got out my wallet and gave Kamezo ten yen.

Shopping street near the Kannon temple

"Here—go and put this in his box," I told him.

That brought the man straight over. "Many thanks," he said, "and God bless you—He won't forget."

As far as I was concerned, the more God forgot the better, and I wondered if I hadn't gone a bit too far for once.

But then I noticed he had these terrible burn scars all over one side of his face. All swollen and purple—you couldn't help feeling sorry for him. He got a card out of his pocket and said, "Please contact me if ever I can be of any help." The card had the Salvation Army address on it, and the man's name: if I remember rightly it said Hashiba somebody or other, and he was a captain in rank. The burn apart, he looked rather distinguished, with a good, strong sort of face. I was impressed; I'd never realized they had that kind of man in his sort of work.

But we'd come out to enjoy ourselves, so we said goodbye and left him, and we hadn't been strolling around long before we'd forgotten all about the Salvation Army. We dropped in at two or three places for a drink and a bite to eat, and got fairly plastered, then I called a cab, sent Kamezo on home, and told the driver to take me across the river to a brothel I knew called Yamaki. But I must have gone to sleep, because before I realized it the driver was saying we were there. Feeling nice and comfortable I hauled myself up, paid the fare, and got out. I then made my way into the waiting room and called for them to bring me a cup of tea.

At this, the madam turns up and wants to know if I've ever been to her place before. So I tell her, rather sharp, that she must be half asleep or something, and not to be so unfriendly.

"No, really," she says, perfectly serious, "this is the first time I've seen you, sir."

I couldn't believe it. So I took another look around me, and something didn't seem to fit. Damned if I hadn't got the wrong place!

"Hey—where exactly *am* I?" I asked.

"Why, at Komonjiro, of course."

"Well, I really have screwed things up! Sorry." And I got up to go.

"But it doesn't really matter, does it?" she said—she was only doing her job, after all. "Maybe it was lucky in a way. So please—why not stay now that you're here?"

"Well, then, perhaps I will...," I said, and popped upstairs.

So I spent the night with one of the girls there called Okyo. But for someone in a place like that she was a real amateur. When I asked her how long she'd been working there, she said only three months. It must be pretty tough, I said. That made her look like she was going to burst into tears, and she began to tell me all about herself, things she'd never told anyone else, apparently. It was—well, a miserable story. But I'd come there for a good time, and I couldn't afford to be too softhearted. So I just kept saying "I see ... oh, yes ... dreadful," and so on, to make her feel better.

But that only made her more serious still. "If only I could get out of here," she said, sitting on the quilt and crying, with this bright-colored shift draped over her shoulders. But what did she expect *me* to do about it? I was in a fix. She seemed to mean business, too, which made it all the more awkward.

So I told her: "OK, listen ... maybe it was fate or something, me coming here, so let's talk about it again next time we meet. Then I'll do whatever I can."

I was just talking, of course—I wasn't planning on going there again, and, after all, she was in the trade, she'd forget all about me as soon as the next man came along. But I was wrong there. You see—it must have been about two months later—she actually came to call on me, bringing another woman with her.

It was in the daytime, around noon, and I was reading the paper in the back room when one of my youngsters came in and said,

"Boss, there are a couple of women out front saying they've come to see you."

"What kind of women?" I asked, puzzled.

"Personally, I'd say they were *that* kind of woman." It was obvious what he meant, but by then I'd forgotten all about Komonjiro and hadn't a clue who "*that* kind of woman" could be. So I told him to show them in, kept them waiting a while, then went out to see them. And, of course, it was the girl I'd been with in the brothel.

"Hey," I said, surprised. "What's up?"

"Well, actually, I came to ask your advice, I thought you might help."

"What is it, then?" I said, and it turned out she'd run away.

"For a while after I saw you I tried to put up with it," she said, "but just then a letter came saying my father was sick and they were in trouble at home. So I asked them if I could go back for a while, but they refused to let me go."

Whenever one of the women in the red-light district went out, a man called a "minder" used to go with her, so usually there wasn't any chance of running away even if the woman wanted to. I asked her how she'd managed it, and she told me that just around that time there'd been a circus in the area.

There was a pond with quite a big open space around it, and the circus had taken over this empty ground for a while. They had all the usual things: elephants and tigers, and trumpets tootling away, and a man at the wicket shouting, "The world's greatest circus! Elephants! Acrobats! Just beginning! Roll up, roll up!" As she and another girl were going past the tents, they found a place where you could see into one of them, and they stopped and watched for a bit. The "minder," too, got wrapped up in it, so she thought: it's now or never. She signaled to the other girl with her eyes, and they ran for all they were worth.

"I get the picture...," I said, feeling this was really awkward. You see, for a prostitute to run away in those days was a full-fledged crime. The brothel keeper had bought the woman for so many hundred yen, and if she ran off before she'd paid it all back the police were called in. Even if she reached her own home, they'd bring her back again, so there was no real point in escaping in the first place.

It put me, too, on the spot. It was out of the question to keep them there at my place, but, seeing them, I hadn't the heart to kick them out, either. I was wondering what the hell to do, when all of a sudden I remembered Captain Hashiba of the Salvation Army.

In those days the Salvation Army had its headquarters in Kanda. They were very keen on the "emancipation" of prostitutes, and they'd already got some quite good results. What they preached was that prostitutes should be free to give up the job if they wanted to. And they spread the idea that women who tried to give up the work should be given protection.

Just the thing, I thought to myself, and I phoned them up right away. Luckily enough, Captain Hashiba was there at the time, and remembered who I was. So I explained the situation and asked him if he couldn't do something.

"That's a very good thing you've done," he said. "I'll come

immediately." And he arrived within the hour. They told him their story, and he listened carefully.

"I see," he said finally. "I'll try to fix things up." The girls bowed happily and said "Please!" and went straight off with him. Later on—several weeks, I suppose it was—Hashiba turned up to say it had been arranged for them to get out, and I wasn't to worry any more, and I was to get in touch if I ever needed him again.

As he was talking, I took a good look at his scarred face, and thought to myself that it takes all kinds to make a world.

Anyway, that's not the end of the story. One day not long before the beginning of the war, the same girl suddenly showed up at my place again. I asked her what the hell she was doing there, and she said she wanted me to give her a job—like that, right out of the blue. "If I stay at home I think they'll sell me off again," she says, "so I've run away."

I asked her a bit more about it, and it seemed her father was a real bastard; I even began to feel I'd have run away *myself* if I'd been in her shoes. As it happened, my wife, Omon, turned up just then and asked what was happening. Omon had a house she used as a school to teach dancing in; she had about ten pupils, and was doing pretty well.

"Listen, why don't you send her to work at my place?" she said.

"But you've got a maid already, haven't you?"

"Yes," she said, "but she's such a slut, I've been thinking I could do with another one as well."

Then she said straight out to the girl: "I'm not easy to please, and I may be a bit of a nag, but if you don't mind that, will you come and try it?"

The girl wasn't in any position to pick and choose. So that

decided it: she went to work at Omon's house.

This was the Okyo that was so helpful to me later on. Seeing that I'd been to bed with her at Komonjiro, I had my doubts about the arrangement, but it didn't seem to bother Omon at all.

The Payroll

About two years before the war, I took over as head of the Dewaya. Strictly speaking, Muramatsu was still boss, but he'd ruined his health with drugs and was in and out of the hospital, so I was left in charge. The trouble was, though, that by then Japan had got itself bogged down in the war with China, business in general was in a slump, and we were feeling the pinch on our side, too.

I told you before—maybe I didn't—that our headquarters was at 1-1 Shinhata-cho, Asakusa. That meant it was slap bang in the middle of the entertainment district, and our territory was one of the best. Even so, good territory doesn't mean you can afford to sit around and take things easy. As they say, every stream has its depths and shallows, and our business is no different. What it boils down to is that you can't win at gambling, or bring in a lot of players, just by willing it. You wonder sometimes why, when you've got a perfectly good gambling joint, everybody goes elsewhere; but it's not something you can explain logically.

And it's just as likely to go the other way, too. I mean, that the right kind of customers can pour in even though you're not putting yourself out to attract them. When that happens, your popularity attracts more people still, and you find yourself doing a roaring trade. Looking back on it now, I can see that the period when I first joined the Dewaya was one of the very best—the money was just rolling in. But maybe I ought to tell you something at least about where the money went to.

In my time, twenty percent was deducted from the day's

191

earnings right at the start. Suppose that on one evening there was an income—by today's reckoning—of ten million yen, we'd set two million aside. Then the boss would take sixty percent of the remainder, and divide the rest among the other men. What about the twenty percent deducted at the beginning, you'll say. Well, first there was the money that went to pay allowances to anyone in jail. Then there were the everyday expenses—they came out of the twenty percent as well.

But what about the sixty percent that went to the boss? It looks like a hefty profit. It wasn't as simple as all that, though: it wasn't as if it went into his pocket and stayed there for him to do what he liked with.

The first thing to remember is that in that trade people, all kinds of them, flock around wherever there's money. It's like having ticks—there are just too many of them for you to shake them all off, however much you try. You find yourself with ten or twenty hangers-on, for a start. These aren't people you've asked to stay with you—they're mostly young gamblers. And they don't bring any cash with them, either; no, they've drifted over because they've heard you were doing well, and so you have to give them something to play with.

If you ask why we do that, it's because among gamblers there's always been a sort of mutual aid system. Well, I don't know whether you could really call it a *system*. Anyway, say you've got ten brothers—ten gambling bosses who've all made a solemn promise to help each other out. Well, it never happens, under any circumstances, that all the gangs are going strong at the same time. If thirty percent are doing fine and thirty percent are getting by, then you can be sure that the other forty will be doing practically no business at all. And that's at normal times, too; when I became the boss in Asakusa, business as a whole was more or less at a standstill, and you could have counted the number of gambling joints making good money in Tokyo on the fingers of one hand. I'd say about a third at most were just struggling along. The rest were "open for no business," as we used to say.

Now, once the customers stop coming, there's nothing you can do about it. You can't make a river flow backwards, and it's the same with them. That's a pretty serious matter, however you look at it—particularly if you've got a lot of men you're responsible for. You're stuck. So what you do is farm some of your guys out with another boss who's doing better. They don't stay there at night, but they hang around during the games, and the boss gives them some pocket money to gamble and buy food with. It wouldn't be right, of course, to dump dozens of them on one single joint, so you divide them up among several. Even so, if there are several bosses in trouble at the same time, the number of guys put out to pasture goes up accordingly, and it gets difficult to look after them all.

With gambling, you never know when you're going to lose your players; just because things are going well at the moment doesn't mean it's going to be the same in a few years' time. So there was a kind of rule that bosses who were doing OK should look after those who weren't. It was quite common for someone who had, say, thirty men of his own to be feeding as many as twice that number. It was tough, but if you couldn't do that much you might as well have quit. There's a yakuza saying that you should be willing to risk your life to give a brother a meal and a night's shelter. In actual practice, though, there's much more to it than that: even at normal times, we were always helping each other out, and whenever some real trouble cropped up we'd make any sacrifice to meet our obligations to each other.

In movies and novels, the yakuza are always reaching for a sword or a gun, but that's just bullshit. Professionals were different in those days. Their job, the job they depended on for a living, was to shake the dice and give their customers a good time, which meant it was actually quite rare for them to quarrel. There were bosses who didn't see eye to eye, of course, but if they'd started carving each other up just because they didn't get on well, the police would have clamped down on them, and their business would have folded. So in a way you could say we were more accommodating generally than ordinary people.

Anyway, what about other expenses? Well, there were things like presents at funerals and when people were sick. These set you back quite a bit. If the boss of some gang or other died, you had to send along a gift of money, on a scale that matched the connection you'd had with him. Or if his wife, say, or a close relative died, you still had to fork out a fairly large amount. Even when some youngster from a brother's gang had finished a spell in jail, it meant another little envelope with cash inside.

The professional outfits all had a kind of ranking inside their own world, and it was up to you to give an amount suited to your own status, too. It wouldn't do to have people saying among themselves: "Look at this miserable little bit the Dewaya have sent—and them always pretending to be so grand." So naturally you tried to make a good showing.

On top of all these business obligations, there were also the local shop and restaurant owners to cope with. It happened all the time in an area like ours: one of them would turn up and say, "Boss—I'm opening a new place at such-and-such an address. I hope you'll watch out for us." And you could hardly ignore it. So you put a bit of money in an envelope and sent one of those big wreathes of artificial flowers they set up in front of any new premises. Then, on the day they actually opened, you'd take along seven or eight of your men to drink to their success and get them off to a good start. You gave tips to the staff, and you went around the customers saying you hoped they'd patronize the place; then, when you thought the right time had come, you thanked the owner and made yourself scarce. But you stayed in touch. And anything like a funeral or a birth meant another wreath or an envelope from the boss—it all added up.

None of our income, though, came from these establishments; apart from some "protection" money, everything we earned was through organized gambling. Anybody who messed around with anything outside that wasn't a real yakuza. Of course, there were always people who *called* themselves yakuza—pimps, for instance, who hung around the red-light districts—but we wouldn't touch them with a bargepole.

People often confused us with the *tekiya*, too, who looked after any kind of outdoor entertainment. There was a *tekiya* boss two doors away from us called Fukuda Tengai. Whenever a circus, say, turned up, the owner would drop in to pay his respects, and Fukuda would get what they called a "cushion charge." This was half the fee they charged each person for the cushions they set out in the circus tents. But, though we were neighbors, he operated independently, and we just left him to it.

The sort of entertainment the yakuza *were* connected with was anything performed under a roof—inside a building, that is. If some place where they usually showed movies or had strip shows decided to put on a play or a recital of some kind, the manager and the head of the troupe would come along and ask for our support. We'd wish them luck, of course, but we'd also give them a little consideration wrapped up in paper. At my place, it was Kamezo who looked after everything in that line. He was a cheerful fellow, and so long as they buttered him up a bit, he was more than willing. "Right," he'd say. "From what day to what day, was it? OK, I'll take care of everything personally; if there's anything that bothers you, just let me know." Anybody in the entertainment world who was going to put on something in Asakusa knew there wouldn't be any trouble if he had the Dewaya's backing.

You might wonder, then, what was in it for us. Well, they didn't pay for our support in money so much as in kind. We did it like this. If the International Theater, for example —which was on our turf—had a new show running for a month, the manager would pop in and say something like: "We're due to open tomorrow—and everything's going smoothly, thanks. We've set the twenty-ninth and thirtieth aside as your days, so we hope you'll come to see us then and get the money for your expenses." What this actually meant was that they'd give the returns for those two days to the Dewaya; if admission fees for the two days came to, say, three million in today's money, we pocketed the lot. It was the same not just in Asakusa but in every territory.

This sounds like good money for doing next to nothing. But no boss worth his salt would ever have let it go at that. He'd accept the days' takings, but then—seeing as he was a sort of short-term promoter—he'd call all the performers together, along with the ticket collectors and stagehands, thank them, and give them all a tip. This was usually more than their normal wages for the two days. Now, if attendance was poor, you still had to give them a decent amount; and if the takings weren't enough to cover it, you had to dig into your own pockets. So it wasn't a bad deal at all the manager was making....

Anyway, what with all these customs and obligations and looking after people and keeping up appearances, the boss of a yakuza gang was bound hand and foot, and however much money came in he never really had enough.

Where the running of the gambling joints themselves was concerned, there were all kinds of carefully worked out arrangements between the different bosses. For example, places not too far apart would always schedule their sessions at slightly different times. There wasn't exactly a fixed timetable, but supposing there were separate joints operating in Uguisudani, Shitaya, and Asakusa, they'd arrange it so that a keen player could take in all three of them. And sometimes one boss would drop in at another place for a game. I say "for a game," but it wasn't just that: he'd do what was called "working the tray"—the "tray" being where the dice were tipped out. And to "work it"—this isn't so easy to explain—meant doing various things to push the game along and get the players really turned on.

Pace is important. A gambling joint depends on the house cut. Suppose the guy running the place—the *domoto*—gets a five percent share of the takings on each game, by the end of the evening he might make five million for himself if they play a hundred rounds. If play goes slowly, though, and there are only fifty rounds, then his income is cut by half. Now, games can get bogged down when the bookie calls "Place your bets!" and somebody starts racking his brains about what to do—it's his money, after all, and he wants to win. At times like that, a boss from another place can help. He'll slap down

197

a wad of money as if it was so much old newspaper and say something like: "Here—which side d'you say is still short? I'll bet on whichever you like. What's all the delay for? You can think about it as long as you like, but you'll never win by thinking!" That's his way of getting the game unstuck—and he'll push through another twenty-five rounds where otherwise it would have stopped at twenty, and your earnings go up accordingly. It's like the men carrying the portable shrine at a festival—they work themselves and everybody else up by shouting "*wasshoi-wasshoi*" until there's a proper festival mood. Once the mood's there, everything's fine: the games race along, and even if the customers lose money, they'll say to you as they leave: "Thanks, I really enjoyed today's session."

A lot of people seem to think that gambling's always crooked, but they couldn't be more wrong. There *are* gamblers who cheat, of course, but the real professionals never do. I mean, think about it. Naturally, you do get newcomers at some games, but there are plenty of old hands, too. So if you didn't play it straight, you'd soon get caught. Word would get around, and people would stop coming, it's as simple as that. So the men running their own joints inside a fixed territory never cheat under any circumstances. The people who *do* cheat are the gamblers who go it alone, without any kind of boss–follower relationships. They don't have any place of their own, and they hold their sessions in a room at an inn or somewhere.

There are dozens of ways of rigging games, but the most common one is to use loaded dice, which you get a professional dice-maker to produce; he'll only do it through a go-between, of course, someone he can trust never to mention his name. This usually involves weighting the dice inside with lead, so that either odd or even numbers tend to turn up more often. The "shooter" then slips the loaded dice into the cup to suit himself, whenever the betting gets one-sided. But there's another special type of dice as well, with powder inside, and a tiny hole. When you shake it, a little bit of the stuff comes out whenever it's at a certain angle—but not enough to notice normally unless you really strain your eyes. At first it's just a perfectly ordinary dice, but as the game progresses its balance is upset, and the spots begin to turn up more odd than even or whatever. Still, it's always best to keep the room dark with that sort of dice. You've had it if anyone notices those specks of dust....

One glance at a player, though, is usually enough to tell you what kind of person he is. Better still, watch how he handles his money. Generally speaking, the loser in life is a loser at dice. He's so keen to win that he can't see how things are as a whole. He dithers over which way to bet, and then bets without looking properly. It's a bit like Sumo wrestlers. If a wrestler feels pressed or uncertain what to do, his body tightens up and won't move as he wants it to; he's lost the bout even before he's put any effort into it. You often see that kind of bout, and you see just the same sort of thing with gambling. A wrestler who's undecided may use his arms, but he can't use his legs properly at the same time. Well, he may use them, but his mind is there before him, and he ends up losing.

Another thing: the professional gambler never worries about where a customer got the money he has to play with. After all, money can't talk, it's just pieces of paper, so you can never tell what he went through to get hold of it. The cash you see him holding in his hand might have come from stripping the quilts off his wife as she lay sick in bed, or by hocking all her kimonos and the sashes with them, but you can't afford to worry about things like that.

There's a line in an old song: "Using the money he sold his missus for." Well, there really *were* men who'd sell their wife to a brothel so they could gamble with the money. It wasn't hard to find a "broker" in those days—the sort that bought and sold women—and a man could just go to one of them and say: "I need some cash. I'll leave the wife with you, so lend me some till tomorrow." "OK," the broker would say. "Let's see now—I reckon she'd fetch"—and he'd name a figure—"so I'll give you half."

But he'd never win with money he'd gone to such lengths to get—he'd lose the lot. So what happened then? "We made an agreement, didn't we?" the other man would tell him, and he'd take his wife off and sell her to a brothel.

As for myself, gambling was my profession, and no matter how much a loser like that cried and begged me to do something, it was none of my business.

Let's face it, gambling is a mug's game. It's like putting an old pestle in an empty mortar and grinding away with it; the pestle gradually gets shorter, till you've got nothing left. Things are arranged that way from the start, so that the money, in the end, is all swallowed up. But you can't stop people hoping their lucky number will come up. It's pretty frightening, really, when you think about it....

Osei

You may remember I made friends in jail with someone called Muraoka, who helped me get started in Uguisudani. Well, a year or two later he went off to Manchuria, but before he left he asked me to keep an eye on his two stepsisters. He'd rented a house for them not far away. Muraoka had a bull neck, a square jaw, and a flattened nose, but both girls were really pretty, and the oldest of them, Osei, was bright as well. She had a way with men ... she'd get a man interested in her, then watch for a chance to duck out of reach, but still keep him dangling on a string. Her timing was perfect.... Neither of them, in fact, really needed any looking after at all.

Anyway, I saw quite a lot of Osei myself over the years. "Uncle," she used to call me. I had a wife by then, of course, but I didn't think of myself as being all that old, so one day I told her not to call me that. What was wrong with "brother," I asked. But she just laughed: "You might take advantage of it," she said. "I'll settle for uncle." And she stuck to it, right to the end.

One time—it was probably still fairly early in the war, because business was lousy around then—I didn't see her for about ten days, then when she did show up she said:

"Uncle—I've got a very special favor to ask."

"What is it," I said, "and why all of a sudden like this?"

"Lend me some money, will you?"

"How much?"

"A thousand yen."

That shook me. It wasn't the kind of sum you asked anyone for lightly. I wanted to know why.

"It's got nothing to do with you," she said. "Just lend it to me and don't ask questions."

"Look, Osei," I told her, "are you trying to make me feel small or something? You know I don't have that kind of money at my place."

For quite a while, in fact, we'd been going through such a rough patch that I hardly had anything available, let alone enough to lend people. Luckily, I'd been able to farm out some of my men elsewhere, so I could just get by, but there was hardly any cash in hand at all. Being a man, I naturally wanted to help out a pretty girl like her, but this was one case where even that was impossible.

So what do you think she said next? She asked me to be a guarantor. The catch was, I was supposed to guarantee a woman—her—being used as security. I'd better explain.

There was a pawnbroker in Asakusa called Marushichi, and Osei had hocked a great pile of kimonos to them for a thousand yen. For a pawnbroker to fork out money like that, the kimonos themselves must have been worth several times that much. Apparently, the reason she'd borrowed such a hefty amount was that there were some goods she wanted to buy up for resale. She didn't tell me as much herself, but I was pretty sure it was black-market stuff. She just couldn't get enough money together, though, so she'd talked about it to a man called Seishichi, a playboy whose father owned a lot of land in Asakusa. It seems she was having an affair with him.

According to Osei, Seishichi had told her: "I could lend it to you easily enough, but that'd be no fun. Why don't we do it like this? There's another pawnbroker called Maruto. If I ask them, I'm sure they'll offer you more for the kimonos than Marushichi did. So the first thing to do is redeem them, then take them and hock them at Maruto."

"Yes, but I don't have any cash," Osei had said, "so how can I get them out of the first place?"

Seishichi laughed. "That's the interesting part. You can pawn *yourself* instead. Then while you're sitting in the cage at Marushichi, I'll take the clothes to Maruto and borrow the money there. If I take them myself, they'll give me a good rate, so I'll bring the money back, pay off Marushichi with interest, and get you back. There—isn't that a good idea?"

It sounded typical of him to me. Only somebody with his time and money to waste could come up with such a hare-brained scheme. His father, too, believed in burning the candle at both ends—he even told me once that he'd cover *any* losses his boy made at my place—so no wonder Seishichi had turned out that way. "Fun" was the name of their game.

"I'm not going to interfere with anything you two want to do," I told Osei, "but Marushichi's always been known as a respectable business. I'm sure they'd refuse to take a woman instead of a normal pledge."

"I know," said Osei. "That's why I want you to help. If only *you* said you'd be my guarantor, they'd hardly be able to refuse. They might not trust *me*, but with you in on it ..."

For one reason or another, and being at a bit of a loose end anyway, I sent for Seishichi and asked him whether he thought he could bring it off.

"Leave it to me, boss," he said. "I swear I won't do anything to embarrass you."

So in the end I agreed, and the three of us went along to Marushichi. The owner, not surprisingly, sounded shocked.

"Nobody does that kind of thing, I'm afraid," he said. "No pawnshop could keep going if it returned goods without getting the money back first."

"I'm sure you're right," I said. "And I know we're asking a

lot. But if we leave Osei here instead, couldn't you let us keep the kimonos for a while?"

That shocked him even more. "Come on, boss, give me a break, will you?" he said. "We deal in things, not bodies."

"Well, then—this may sound weird, and it makes *me* look a fool, at least—but couldn't I be the pledge while Osei's here? That'd be good enough, surely?"

"You must be joking. It'd scare all my customers away, having a boss like you hanging around the shop.... Still ... you must have pretty good reasons for going as far as that. OK, then: I'll give you back the goods. But make sure you bring in the money before the day's out."

So he gave way in the end, and brought out all the kimonos. Osei, to make it look right, went and sat inside the cage behind the counter. Then Seishichi disappeared with the bundle of clothes, and got Maruto to pay up on the spot.

He'd known what he was talking about, boasting that he could take care of everything: I found they'd lent him two thousand yen. I mean, two thousand—a ridiculous amount! I reckon it was his reputation more than the actual value of the stuff that did it. Anyway, we gave Marushichi their money back with interest, and Osei did what she wanted to with the extra cash. She used it on some black-market deal, that's for certain. And she must have made quite a bit on it, too, because it wasn't long before she'd got her kimonos back from Maruto as well.

One thing that showed she'd made a decent profit was this. I suppose it was a month or two after the pawnshop business, and I was still kicking my heels; I couldn't organize any games, because you need customers for that, and there weren't any. So one day I took my last hundred yen in ready cash and went to play at a place run by a boss called Gen-chan, in Senju.

But you're never lucky at times like that. Before I knew what hit me, I'd lost it all. As I was sitting there feeling disgusted with myself, Gen-chan came up and said: "You haven't got warmed up yet. How about another try?" Unlike some of us, he was doing pretty well in those days, and there were at least fifty men in the room.

I was tempted—it's hard to leave without trying to recoup your losses after you've been asked to play another round —but, as I told him, the cash just wasn't there.

"Come on," he said, "you don't need to say that kind of thing!" And he had someone bring me a wad of bills. There was five hundred yen there when I checked.

But my luck was out, and that went the same way as the first: straight down the drain. So he lent me some more. He did the same thing a couple more times, in fact; and I blew the lot.

So I thanked him, told him I'd pay him back tomorrow, and left. But I was in quite a state, I can tell you. I hadn't just lost, I'd lost *eight hundred yen*. I couldn't possibly scrape up that much money.

I went home feeling pretty sick, then sat down and did some hard thinking. The boss of the Dewaya couldn't just say "Look, I'm sorry, I'm broke, so let me off." And he couldn't run for it, either—it would have made a laughingstock of him.

I was racking my brains there, leaning against the charcoal brazier and poking at the ash with the tongs, when I heard a voice behind me. It was Osei.

"What are *you* doing here?" I asked.

"That's a fine way to welcome a woman," she said. "What's

up?" And she looked at me closely.

"Nothing."

"I don't believe a word of it. Something's wrong, isn't it?"

Osei was pretty sharp, you know. She could tell at a glance that I was in trouble. It was no use trying to hide it, so I said,

"Oh, it's nothing much, I just lost every game I played today."

"How come? I thought you were an expert." But she looked sympathetic, all the same.

"Gen-chan said he'd lend me some more money, so I was fool enough to take it—and then I went and lost that, too."

"Wow. How much was it?"

Well, I didn't have anyone else to talk to, and I was feeling low. At times like that, you're glad of somebody you can at least tell the facts to without worrying, so I ended up coming clean: told her how much I'd taken with me, how much I'd borrowed, and so on.

"I see," she said, cool as a cucumber. "Uncle, listen—let me take care of it."

That annoyed me. "We're not talking about pin money, Osei, this is serious."

She didn't turn a hair. "But you're broke, aren't you? How do you think you're going to get it?"

"That's just what I'm thinking about right now."

"Well, then, let me do the thinking for you. I mean— you've helped me no end in the past...."

I wasn't sure how seriously to take her. "All right," I grumbled, "if that's how you feel about it, perhaps I'll try leaving things to you for once."

"Right!" she said. "I'll be back soon, so stay put there."

A few hours later she was back.

"Here you are, then," she announced, unwrapping a bundle tied up in a cloth. There was a whole pile of money inside.

"For shit's sake, Osei. Where did you get so much?"

"Does it matter?" she said, just as calm as ever. "You wouldn't be any the wiser if I told you. Just use it."

"Well, thanks, I mean it! I'll take it as a loan."

The next morning I told Omon, my wife, and had a couple of my guys take the money to Gen-chan in Senju. That way I managed somehow to save face. If it hadn't been for Osei, I don't see how I could have carried on working as a yakuza.

As it turned out, though, this episode led to a bit of personal trouble. My wife got jealous. As she saw it, for Osei to lend me all that money must mean that we were lovers. She'd never complained about the way Osei came and went at our place, but all the while inside her she must have been holding it against me, so that it exploded over this business of the loan.

There was a nasty scene. She looked as if she wanted to scratch my eyes out.

"Borrowing money from a woman like that—you'll ruin the Dewaya's reputation. Gen-chan asked me all kinds of things—I was so *ashamed*!"

"What—you mean you told him where the money came from?"

"Of course not! Who d'you take me for? But you've handled it all wrong from the start. Why did you keep *me* in the dark about it? You might not think it, but I'm your *wife*! If you'd just told me how things stood, we could have found the money somehow, even if it meant selling the house and land. And if that still wasn't enough, *I* could have managed it somehow—why, I'd have sold myself if I had to! But you—*you* have to keep it quiet, then go and borrow it from that bitch."

Her face was as white as a sheet.

"I didn't go and ask Osei," I explained; "she just happened to turn up when I was thinking about it."

"That's not the point!" she said. "With something as important as that, why didn't you tell me straightaway?"

"I wanted to, but, honestly, what could you have done about it?"

"I *said* I'd sell myself, didn't I?"

"Oh, for God's sake! How do you think *I'd* look if I sold my own wife because I couldn't pay my debts?"

By the end of it, neither of us was making any sense. So I told her she was a fool, then stormed out and didn't come back for two or three days. When I did, I found she'd packed up all her stuff and left. Didn't come back for some time, either. Anyway, it was my fault for losing the money in the first place, so I let a month go by, then apologized and got her to come home. But things were never the same after that, and we ended up separating.

Sometime during the war, Osei asked if she could come and live on the second floor of the house; and since this was OK with me, she became a member of the household, along with Okyo—the girl Captain Hashiba had rescued—and five or six of my own men. She wasn't there every day, though: she'd stay for a couple of days, then disappear for a while. She never said where she'd been to, and I didn't ask. Just because she was in the same house didn't mean we were living together as man and wife, so it wasn't any business of mine what she did. I don't know how it looked to other people, but I never even slept with her—not once.

One clue as to what she was up to came when she turned up one day with a laborer pulling a handcart and asked if she could leave some stuff upstairs. They carried in a good twenty or thirty containers about the size of gasoline cans. I was wondering what they were, when Osei told me: white sugar. It was hard to get hold of sugar of any kind around that time, so white sugar was fairly valuable. I expect she'd bought up a lot somewhere and was hoping to sell it at a much stiffer price; either way, she didn't discuss it with me at all. After a while she must have found a customer, because they loaded it onto a handcart again, all except two cans, and carried it away. I took that to mean—not that I had any real grounds for it—that they'd left a couple of cans by way of thanks, and we used them, they came in very handy.

Osei disappeared without a word. That was the last I saw of her until a while after the end of the war, though I heard later that she'd been in Kobe. It was due to Osei that I went to jail in Abashiri, seven or eight years after the defeat, but I'll tell you about that later.

IV

I finished taking his blood pressure, and snapped the top off an ampoule in order to give him an injection.

"That sound always takes me back," he said with quiet feeling as he lay there between the quilts. "My old boss was forever having the doctor in to examine him, and the doctor, after he'd looked him over, would snap the top off those things in just that way. I'd be standing close by, and I can still hear the sound even now."

"How's your appetite?"

"Not too bad. But when your legs start swelling up, it means you're near the end of the road, doesn't it?... Come to think of it, though, people looked even puffier than me during the war, didn't they?—in the face at least."

A brief smile flashed across his cheeks, which were mapped with dark brown blemishes, and without getting up he put a cigarette which the woman had lit for him between his lips.

"Were you in Tokyo all through the war?" I asked.

"No. I got out into the country toward the end."

"Where did you go?"

"Kashiwa. There was a transit camp nearby, and there was plenty going on to keep us interested."

He blew out an appreciative puff of smoke, handed the rest of the cigarette back, and turned on his side.

"Shall I make your pillow a bit higher?" the woman asked.

"No, leave it.... Listen, doctor—how much longer do you give me?"

"It depends on how well you take care of yourself."

"Let's not beat about the bush. What you really mean is around two or three months, isn't it?"

213

"No, I don't. You're good for another two or three years yet."

He laughed. "You're only half my age, but you've still got what it takes. Doctors have to be like you. Perhaps I shouldn't say this, but doctors and gamblers are surprisingly alike in some ways."

"You think so?"

"Yes, I do. A patient may think he's done for, but the doctor will talk him into taking his medicine just the same. The customers at a gambling place know they're going to lose, but they let themselves be taken in by the professional's smooth talk, and end up making heavy bets. It's just a fact. I suppose that's how people manage to keep going: life would be pretty grim if everything went according to the rule book. Look at me—so long as I believe I've got a while left like you say, doctor, I expect I'll find the energy to do it somehow."

Pork and Bombs

One day—it was before the air raids really started—Okyo came up with a suggestion: why not try making a bit of extra money by selling black-market pork?

"Even high-class restaurants are having a hard time nowadays because they can't get hold of meat," she said. "They're only too glad to buy it at any price."

Okyo had stayed on as a maid even after I'd separated from Omon; she was a marvel, saw to absolutely everything for me. While the old boss of the Dewaya was still alive, they'd never employed any women, either at the gambling joint or in the boss's house; but we weren't so strict about it. A sign of the times, I suppose. In the old days, it would have been unthinkable for a woman to tell the head of a gang to consider a sideline of that kind.

Anyway, Kamezo had his doubts about it. "But where do *we* find the meat?" he wanted to know.

"I've got relatives in the country, down in Chiba," said Tokuji, one of our old hands. "They keep pigs. We could get them to let us have some." He seemed surprisingly keen on the idea. He and Okyo had been planning to get married for some time, and I expect they'd got it all worked out in advance together.

But Kamezo still didn't look convinced. "Just knowing a farmer doesn't make it any easier," he said. "If the military police got wind of the fact you'd killed pigs without permission and sold them on the black market, you'd be really in the shit."

He was right, too: you couldn't do anything with farm animals without permission. Military needs had absolute priority, and it was a serious offense to kill a pig secretly and eat or sell the meat. But Tokuji talked as if he knew what he was up to, and told us not to worry. So I let him go ahead, warning him to watch his step, and to leave *me* out of it altogether.

The number of gambling places shutting shop because of the war was increasing steadily, but just around then I began to get some customers, including a few *tekiya* bosses and their men. One of them was a guy called Katano, a brother of mine who had a lot of clout. The *tekiya* were well into the black-market business by then, including meat, and Katano and Tokuji, with his wife-to-be, must have talked it over. Anyway, he was all for the idea. He had good contacts, so they soon found a lot of outlets, and the meat sold well. The porters were kept busy: every three days or so they'd dump a whole load of meat in cans on our second floor. Even cans were hard to come by at the time, and when there weren't any available, they'd put the stuff in greaseproof paper and wrap it around their bellies. They came by train, then trolley, and did the last stage on foot. Thinking back on it, it's a wonder so many of them got away with it.

Even so, just as business was really beginning to go smoothly, there was a hitch, a big one: Tokuji was nabbed by the military police.

His family lived in Chiba, and one day a letter came from them.

"Not often you get a letter," I said.

"It's nothing to worry about," he told me, "but it seems there's been a bit of trouble at home, and I'd like to go and see them."

He set off for his parents' place immediately—but he never

came back. Not a word from him, even, and I was wondering what was wrong when I got word from the MPs that he was dead. It was so sudden, it took a while to sink in, but I soon found out what had happened.

The letter from Tokuji's father had had a notice in it telling him to report for war work. In those days, they were mobilizing ordinary civilians for work in war supply factories, where they turned out airplane parts and shells, sewed parachutes, and so on. These were people like middle school students, who were too young to be conscripted, or women college students, or men who were too old to carry a gun.

Tokuji, though, decided to drop out of sight. Judging from the way he rushed off without saying anything to me, he must have felt discussing it wouldn't do any good. He drifted around Tokyo, Yokohama, and elsewhere, stopping in at friends' houses and sometimes getting the local yakuza to let him have a game. After he died, I heard from people I knew here and there that he'd dropped in on them.

So he drifted on from place to place, until one day he was holed up at a gambling joint in Senju. By sheer bad luck there happened to be a police raid that day, and every single player was rounded up, Tokuji along with them. When they searched him, they found the official summons in his pocket.

I wonder why he hung on to it. Maybe he was thinking of the kid that Okyo was carrying, and told himself that he'd go and report eventually. Anyway, he was done for. Seeing as he was a sort of draft-dodger, the police could hardly not check up on him. They informed the military police, and he was placed in custody at their headquarters in Yokosuka.

I don't know what kind of interrogation they put him through. What's certain, though, is that he got very rough treatment. As they saw it, I suppose, he was the worst sort of slacker—not just shirking his duty but gambling, of all things, at a time when everybody else, as they said in those days, "was united in a battle that would decide the fate of the nation." So they tortured him, till in the end they killed him.

When they told us to come and pick up the body, I decided to take only Kamezo with me. I had a hard job persuading Okyo to stay behind, but if she'd started howling and screaming in front of them, they might have decided to poke around in *our* affairs. For all I knew, as well, Tokuji might have broken down under torture and talked about the black-market business or the gambling, in which case we'd all have been arrested, too. So we left Okyo at home.

"He just got sick and died," they had the nerve to tell us when we turned up. "He said he wanted his body to be left with you. We'll take it to your place in a truck if you'll show us the way."

"Got sick and died"...! I took one look at him and knew he'd been tortured—bad enough to leave his face all twisted out of shape, and bruises all over his body. Still, if we'd looked shocked we'd have been hauled off ourselves on some trumped-up charge, so we just thanked them and climbed on board. It seemed Tokuji hadn't said a word about us.

We got an undertaker to put him in a coffin, offered up some incense for him, then fetched a priest we knew to say a service for him. Okyo, incidentally, held up pretty well. I don't know how she was when she was alone, but in front of other people she didn't even cry.

The next day we took the body to be cremated at a local place. We had papers from the military police saying he'd died of illness, and when we showed them to the people there they did it free of charge. Then we selected some of the ashes and went down to Chiba to hand them over to his parents.

Well, time went by. Japan began to lose the war, and Tokyo started being bombed. In the summer of 1944, we set up what we called the "Two-Seven Circle." It was for gambling, of course: we held sessions on dates with a two or a seven at the end of them, which meant six times a month. The customers were people who owned their own firms in Tokyo and round about—people we could trust to keep their mouths shut. We'd take them to an inn by the sea in Ibaraki prefecture, and let them play in peace and quiet for a while.

When I sent one of my men over to tell them about a session, he'd take along tickets for the train there and back, and a small present as well. Then, when they left after the game, we'd give them something to take home with them—some pork or fish or whisky, say, or shellfish boiled in soy, dried plaice, or sesame oil—things that were in short supply. That impressed them, and we got a pretty good class of customer.

One thing that was helpful in providing presents for them was that Hatsuyo—that's my present wife, I was already having an affair with her at the time, though she was still a geisha then—anyway, she came from a fishing village called Isohama in Ibaraki, and her elder brother was a boatbuilder. When I first asked him if he couldn't get hold of some fish or something, he said, "Right! No problem at all."

All the young men were away in the forces, and all the fishing boats, even the little wooden ones, had been taken over by the military, so almost the only people left in the village were women and old folk. It must have been tough for the women in particular, with no husbands to back them up, but they made what they could by fishing with nets, or diving for abalone, and selling their catch in town. Then, just as they were looking around for something more profitable, who should turn up but us. They were just as pleased as we were, and they brought us a steady supply of dried fish, different kinds of seaweed, octopus, squid, scallops, and so on. Of course, these were all officially off the market, so they were breaking the law.

I remember they used to cook the abalone in soy sauce and make it up into eight-pound packages, dozens of them, which they'd bring around. Normally you couldn't buy them in Tokyo for love or money, so they were fetching thirty yen a package. Now, that's expensive, when you think that the monthly salary of a man who'd been to college was around fifty yen at the time. But with our games bringing in thousands of yen at every session, we weren't going to quibble over the price of a few abalone.

Anyway, we paid the women about twice as much as they could get anywhere else, and we got the pick of the bunch. They brought us plaice, as well—big ones, a good two feet long, and fat, because the fishermen were all away and they had time to grow. It can't have been easy to hide them from the policeman on the bridge they had to cross to get to our inn.

For once, my own business was doing so well that I actually had trouble finding somewhere to keep the profits. If I told you how much we made, you probably wouldn't believe me. But I couldn't put it in the bank, and, times being what they were, there wasn't much to spend it on, either. It just went on piling up.

Okyo's kid was literally brought up on wads of money. You remember those big bamboo baskets they used to have at the public bath in the old days, the ones you put your clothes in? Well, we used to put piles of ten-yen bills in one of those, then lay Masako down to sleep on them. They were soft and springy, and she slept well. Sometimes she'd wet herself, you know, and we'd use the spoiled bills to light the fire under the bath with.

Still, while we were having it easy, the war situation was getting worse and worse, and in the end we decided to move out to Kashiwa, just northeast of Tokyo. Nowadays it's pretty built up around there, from what I hear, but back then it was real country, with no town to speak of at all. We rented a big house standing in the middle of the fields, and went to live there—me and Kamezo, and Okyo and her baby.

Village scene

Even in those days I still had seven or eight men left, though they were all a bit long in the tooth. And we kept up the Two-Seven Circle, right on into 1945 when things were getting really rough, with air raids every day. I remember the twelfth of February, around the beginning of spring. When I arrived at the inn where we held our sessions, the manager said to me:

"We've had it, boss."

"What d'you mean?" I said.

"Japan's just about finished." He was looking more down-in-the-mouth than I'd ever seen him. According to him, there'd been a big B29 raid two days earlier, enough planes to turn the sky black, and Tokyo had been beaten to a pulp.

His assistant was looking pale, too. "We'd better stop the games, with things the way they are," he said.

Well, I wasn't any happier about the B29s than they were, but I didn't see much point in packing up and hiding down a hole. It was carpet bombing; they flattened everything—ordinary houses, hospitals, the lot.

The assistant went on mumbling, till Kamezo spoke up. "Look," he said, "I know some people—there was an air raid, so they all went into the shelter. There was a great shower of incendiaries and the house was burned down, but the shelter survived. They didn't come out again, though. So the neighbors went and looked—and found every one of them dead, done to a turn. You might as well die doing something you enjoy. Come on, then—let's play, and to hell with them."

That cheered the manager up, and we decided to carry on. Then, on February 16, there was another terrific raid. This time they came over low in the sky: carrier-based planes, raking everything with machine guns and scattering incendiaries. Almost none of our planes went up to meet them, so they could do just as they liked.

The biggest of the Tokyo raids came on March 10, and from then on there were machine-gun attacks by carrier planes almost everywhere. The big Hitachi works weren't far away from us at Katsuta; these were attacked in June, and more than a thousand people were killed. The planes were small fighter-bombers, so it looked as if there was a carrier

222

somewhere close. Even so, we didn't close down the Two-Seven Circle: we were past caring by then.

But then one morning, on July 17, something new happened. The game had just got into its stride when there was this low rumbling noise in the distance, like someone dragging a big millstone around. And it kept on coming. It was a deep, heavy kind of crunching that made you feel uneasy just to hear it. And then came the sound of horses—neighing, rushing around in a panic—from an open space quite near the inn where the army kept a number of them. Everybody half got up, then stopped there with the money in their hands, waiting. The rumbling got worse, and the next minute there was an almighty crash, as though the sky'd fallen in.

"That was over by the station, wasn't it?" somebody said. There was a Hitachi arms factory near the station.

"Something blew up, I'd say."

"No. More likely we're making some new weapon to flatten the Yanks with, and they've started testing it."

Surely no gun would kick up a row like that, people were just saying, when that awful rumbling started up again, followed by another great crash that turned your belly inside out. This time there was *really* something wrong, no mistake about it. It wasn't any use putting on a brave face, pretending it was nothing—the sound would have put the wind up anyone. And it came again, and again, another fifteen or sixteen times.

"What the hell is it?"

"You know—it *could* be an enemy battleship."

"You're right. Yes, they're shelling us from the sea."

Everybody turned pale. So this is it, I thought, the American fleet's coming ashore.

"There's nothing we can do about it, anyway," I said, trying to cheer them up. "If there's a direct hit, it'll be the same whether you're in bed or up." So we all moved into the inn's biggest room and drank our way through several crates of saké.

It *was* offshore shelling, as it turned out; and they'd even been able to hear it deep in the mountains off to the west. A great fleet of ships—I don't know whether they were battleships or cruisers—came sailing south, shelling the coast all the way. What was heartbreaking about it was that while they were slamming shells into our towns, not one of our own ships had been around....

Before long, the war was over. But we went on gambling, right to the end.

Free-for-all

The man was lying flat between the quilts. The bright rays of a late winter sun were falling on the windowpanes. Inside the room, the kettle on the stove gave off a faint, soft plume of steam, and from the kitchen at the back came the sound of someone chopping something on a board.

"A patient gave it to my father," I was saying. "One single apple. But I felt it would be a waste to eat it. So I left it on a shelf in the kitchen and gazed at it every day. In the end, of course, it went bad. I was only four at the time, but I remember I was so upset I cried."

The man lay there, looking through half-closed eyes, listening with apparent pleasure.

"Anyway," I went on, "where were you after the war?"

"I stayed in Kashiwa for a while. I mean, things were hopeless in Tokyo."

"Did you organize any gambling?"

"Yes. All kinds of people turned up to play, you'd be surprised. With a lot of them, you had no idea what they did for a living. Some of them, even, stayed for a month or two. There were two who later got on in the world, became town councillors. They're still in office now, so I can't tell you their names."

The beams of sunlight swayed in the steam, and, off and on, the sound of children playing on the riverbank could be heard.

"By the way," he said, "have you ever been to a geisha party?"

"A lot of my patients are former geisha. Most of them are in their seventies or eighties by now. Why do you ask, anyway? Are there any particular geisha you remember?"

"Of course, lots of them. Tsuchiura wasn't too far away, and it being a naval base, you found some real beauties there." He gave a

sidelong glance at the woman by his bed as he spoke.

It wasn't long after the end of the war. I'd been having a game at a friend's place in Tsuchiura, and I'd won some money, so I went to a geisha house. When the girls came in, there was one who was really stunning.

"What's that girl's name?" I asked the guy running the show.

"Ah. You've got a good eye, boss," he said, "—just as I'd expected. Her name's Kofuji, and she's the girl that Yamamoto Isoroku, the commander of the Combined Fleet, took a fancy to when he was here in his younger days."

I was kind of tickled by the idea that this was the woman the head of the whole navy had had an affair with. Anyway, that day I left without doing more than talk a bit with her. But somehow I couldn't get her out of my mind. So I went there pretty often after that. One day, she said to me:

"Boss, there's a favor I'd like to ask.... You see, I want you to take care of a sword for me."

"Funny thing for a geisha to ask a yakuza to do, isn't it? What's this all about?"

"Apparently it's a Bizen sword," she said, perfectly serious still. "It scares me, and I don't want it lying around."

"You've certainly got something on your hands there! They're valuable, those things."

"I had a hundred of them until a while ago, but I got rid of all the rest."

I was shocked. "I could understand, say, two or three," I said, "but—a hundred! Where the hell did you get hold of them?"

So she explained.

Around the time the war ended and naval officers were

226

due to be discharged and sent home, there were various rumors going around about the occupation forces. One was that women would be raped, and it'd be safer if they shaved their heads. Another was that anyone caught with a sword on them would be arrested and shot. Well, it seems a lot of officers believed this story and just chucked their swords away, dumped them in a river or something. But some of them had swords by famous swordsmiths, and rather than lose them altogether, they got the idea of leaving them somewhere safe and getting them back later. That way, a number of officers came to see Kofuji and ask her to look after the things. The Bizen sword was one of them. It had been in the man's family for generations; his grandfather had carried it into battle against the Russians. He told her before he left for home that she was to get rid of it if he didn't come back for it within three years, but not before.

"My place was completely cluttered up with swords. And you know, it's strange, but I kept feeling chilly with them in the house."

"I wonder why, though?" I said a bit doubtfully.

"It's true."

"And so?"

"So, late one afternoon, I found this farmer in the alley outside, and gave him some money to put the swords in the box he used for collecting scraps of pig feed."

"I bet he was pleased, wasn't he?"

"He'd have been in trouble if he was found out, so he piled the scraps on top of them."

The idea made me laugh. "Good for him!" I said. "But what about the Bizen sword—you didn't get rid of that?"

"I was going to, but I couldn't bring myself to somehow."

"So you want *me* to look after it for you, eh?"

"If you wouldn't mind."

"But what'll you do if the officer comes back?"

"I'll tell him the Americans took it away. After all, the kind of man who'll leave a family treasure with a geisha just because he's afraid the Americans might catch him doesn't *deserve* to have it back, does he?"

She had a point there. After I'd agreed to take it off her hands, I got an expert to have a look at it, and he said it was a fine piece of work. He wouldn't name a figure, though, so it must have been quite valuable. I kept it around till only recently, but as there wasn't much sense in keeping a sword at my age, I sold it to an antique dealer. I got a good price for it, too.

One of the "big spenders" at our games in those days was a guy called Tsukada Saburo, and his story's worth telling you. I suppose it would have been about two months after the defeat that he first turned up. He came in carrying a big cloth bundle of money slung over his shoulder. Kamezo pointed him out to me.

"What do you think he is?" he said, looking worried. "Not one of *those*, I hope." And he crooked his finger in the sign for a thief.

But when you heard what Saburo had to say for himself, you felt that "thief" didn't do him justice. He was the kind of man, in fact, who makes you want to take your hat off to the human race. I mean, the way they won't let anything keep them down for long.

He was the seventh son of a greengrocer, but he was turned out of home when he was still a kid. After that, he tried his hand at all sorts of jobs, and ended up a rickshaw man. That was just before the war. But since he only stood about four foot seven and was kind of scrawny, he was never called up. In due course, though, he was mobilized for war work, and the place they sent him was the naval air base at Tsuchiura.

A bunch of us were sitting there listening to him when he told us all about it.

"You ever been inside the base?" he asked me.

"I've been past it in the train, but never inside."

"You wouldn't understand what happened unless you'd actually seen inside. It was the biggest supply depot in the country. You name it, they had it. And within two weeks of the end of the war the whole lot had disappeared. I mean, *vanished*—without a trace."

According to him, it was the Emperor's broadcast—the one announcing the defeat—that started it all off.

"It made thieves of everybody," he said. "There were some, of course, who wept and wailed about it, but most people were as pleased as punch. Up till then, you couldn't so much as fart without written permission for some high-up, but now it was first come, first served. And there was this treasure trove right under their noses, waiting to be cleaned out before the Yanks got to it.

"It started with things like blankets and parachute material. They were falling over each other, dragging it out in great bundles and taking it home. The parachute stuff was silk, and worth its weight in gold. You had to be a fool not to try and nick your share."

But that was only the beginning. Before long, he said, it wasn't just the civilian workers and NCOs, but anyone else who'd heard that since the defeat you could get into the base without a special pass.

"They came in swarms, like ants. They barged into one

warehouse after another—whichever was nearest—grabbed whatever came to hand, put it on carts, and hauled it off.

"The bigger things took a bit of organizing. What happened was, the local big shots used the name of some organization—the Agricultural Co-op or something—and applied to the Supplies Department for an official transfer of property. Not that the department had much clout by then, but they must have been on the take as well, and stamped the documents for them. So naval trucks were made available, and carried off loads of heavy stuff....

"In Takatsu," he told us, "they'd dug deep tunnels in the cliffs, and when the raids got bad the navy shifted tons of food there to keep it safe. I was around when this was going on, so I knew where it was, and so did the people in the neighborhood. And under cover of night, they 'evacuated' it themselves—left the place as clean as a whistle, apparently.

"Evacuating" military stores

"Some of these supplies, in fact, were already in ordinary people's homes. The military had taken over civilian storehouses to keep their own supplies in, a bit in each place —clothes, blankets, canned food, machine tools, etc. Well, with the end of the war, the original owners sort of disappeared, and nobody saw anything wrong with helping himself to them.

"There was masses of timber in the depot, too. Forests were requisitioned during the war—leaving most of our hillsides bare as a result. They used some of the wood to build boats and so on, but a lot of it was left over. So the navy turned it into charcoal and rationed it out to the families of NCOs and above.

"I knew about this," he said, "because while the war was still on, I'd been in charge of the men making the charcoal. I had three kilns built outside the base, and we produced bales and bales of it—good oak and beech charcoal that you'd never get in most households at the time.

"Being an insider, there wasn't much I didn't know about how the other half—the officers—lived. Like what went on in the galleys, as they called them. They had everything: meat, fish, vegetables, piles of the stuff. I was always trying to lift a bit of their grub and give it to the women workers at the base. Lots of them were just middle school girls, you know; they barely got enough to eat in their own homes, and they were stunned when they heard about all that meat."

Another luxury the officers had was coal briquets. Heaps of coal had been commandeered from the mines—more than they could ever use—but as there was nowhere in ordinary houses where you could burn coal directly, it had to be turned into briquets.

"One day," Saburo went on, "this lieutenant in Supplies sent for me and said he'd give me twenty men to do the briquet-making work. I'd put 'briquet manufacturer' down as

231

one of my trades in the form I'd given them, so he must have thought he was onto a good thing.

"Well, making things is just my line—I can even make babies with other men's wives!—and this was a cinch for me. First you powdered the coal, then made a paste out of it with water and a bit of clay. Since the clay wasn't enough to make it set hard, we used to mix in a kind of seaweed called Ise laver as well. After that, all you had to do was shape it and dry it, and you'd got your briquets.

"But there was a limit to the number we could turn out. I knew an ironworks in Chiba, though, where they made briquet-producing machines. So I told the lieutenant about it and suggested he order one; that way, he could keep all the officers supplied, I said.

"He agreed right away. So I went down there and told them what I wanted; but they said they didn't make them any more, nobody was buying them. 'I know,' I said, 'but orders are orders, so do what you can, and just name your price.'

" 'Well,' they said, 'we *could* do it, but it'll cost you seventy thousand.' A hell of a price. But I told them OK, go ahead—it wasn't *my* money, after all. And for two whole days they gave me the red-carpet treatment, with geisha laid on ... I couldn't walk straight for a week.

"A while later, word came that it was ready, so I went to the lieutenant to get the money. But all he gave me was a requisition order, no cash, and when I turned up in Chiba with it, the poor factory owner just burst into tears. You see, with one of those orders, you could walk off with anything—cars, cows, horses, boats, anything—just by handing over a slip of paper. And if anyone objected, they put the MPs onto him.

"After all the wine, women, and song I'd had at their expense, I felt bad about it, but there wasn't anything I could do. I got them to help me load it on the truck, and took it away. And it worked: it turned out thirty briquets at a time. I was impressed; the officers' wives were pleased; and the lieutenant was plain delighted—told me that on the battlefield I'd have been decorated for it...."

"Was there really all that much stuff at the base?" Okyo said, putting her head on one side as if she had trouble believing him.

"There was! Oh yes, they made a packet out of what they stole."

"If I'd known, I'd have gone along myself," somebody else put in. And they all looked as if they'd missed out on something.

"That's what I said, didn't I?—anybody who didn't join in was a fool. But you know—*real* thieves are in a different class. We had a few of them as well." Saburo stared around at everybody and took a swig of his tea.

"The biggest of the lot was the lieutenant himself. He was a real quick-change artist. Almost overnight, he got rid of everything to do with the navy—his epaulets, his sword, his cap. Then he called everybody of foreman rank together and told us: 'As you know, this air depot, like everywhere else, has got to wind up business before the Americans arrive. I need your cooperation. You'll all be wanting to get home as soon as possible yourselves, so from now on I'm going to pay you a daily allowance of five hundred yen.'

"That made everyone rub their eyes. I mean, till then our salaries had been thirty yen a *month*. There were about fifty men of our rank, and we all jumped at the offer. What the actual work involved was loading heavy stores onto trains. There were plenty of sidings inside the base, and every morning dozens of freight cars came in for us to load.

"Mostly it was steel plates, brass, sheets of copper, duralumin, and other alloys—high-grade stuff they used for making aircraft axles and so on. There was masses of tin as well, in bars the shape of bricks. As I found out later, one of them alone would have fetched thousands on the black market. Anyway, the loads were so heavy they made the springs sag if we shoved in anything over a quarter of the car's capacity.

"The trouble was that, like a fool, I thought it was going off to be handed over to the occupation authorities. But I was wrong. The bastards in charge knew it was worth too much for that. They'd worked out that if they got it hidden away before the Americans came, then sold it on the black market, they could make a fortune. And there we were, slaving away to make it easy for them."

"You mean, you did the work without knowing what they were up to?" one of us asked.

"Yep. We were soft—we followed the lieutenant's orders. Just went on loading till the warehouses were empty."

There was a groan from everybody in the room.

"You really don't know where they hid the stuff?" I asked, feeling a bit suspicious.

But Saburo took it in his stride. "If I did, you'd have heard about it," he said. "You could have bought all Hokkaido and Kyushu with that much stuff. So if I had any leads, I would've asked you to help track it down....

"At any rate, payday came around at the end of August, and the lieutenant brought along this orange crate full of money. He took it out in bundles and handed it around. We were thrilled, of course—looking back on it, we must have been real dopes. You see, it was military scrip, issued by the navy. Not real money

—pay for the troops, except there weren't any troops left."

"Wow," said Kamezo admiringly, with his arms folded across his chest. "That lieutenant of yours had brains."

"I know—*we* weren't any match for him. He'd been to the Imperial University, so he was *supposed* to be bright.... Anyway, I was furious. But you never know when your luck's going to change, do you? Not long afterward, I was sitting on a pile of firewood, eating my lunch, when along comes the head of the Accounts Department, on horseback, having a look around. 'Here, Tsukada,' he says, all high and mighty, 'if there's anything you need, just let me know.'

" 'Fuck you,' I felt like telling him. 'You take all the best for yourself, and *then* get generous.' But I managed to keep it to myself and said 'Well, major, I'd like a truck really, but I haven't got a permit.'

"So he grins and says 'That can be arranged. I'll tell the transport section. How many do you want?' 'Four, please,' I say. 'Right,' he says, not turning a hair.

"Well, they gave me the permit—said the major had authorized it. So I dashed off on my bike and relieved the transport pool of four charcoal-burning trucks, then went straight off and called the ironworks in Chiba.

" 'I've got that briquet machine,' I told the owner, 'so come and get it. Be quick about it, or someone else'll pinch it!'

"The next day, he and one of his people came over on bicycles. The machine was already loaded on a truck. Their eyes almost popped out of their heads when I told them they could have the truck as well. 'Take it in return for the night with the geisha,' I said. 'I'll never forget this as long as I live,' the owner answered, with tears running down his cheeks. And off he drove, waving to me as he went. It was funny, really—all

235

that fuss over something I'd swiped myself.

"After that, I used the other trucks to make off with everything I could lay my hands on. Not being the lieutenant, I let everybody who helped me have their cut, so I wasn't short of helping hands. In my case, though, it wasn't just the depot stuff I was after: I knew where they'd stashed supplies in the hills and in bunkers here and there. But it was a race against time. We kept at it day and night, and it went so well that just before we all split up, I decided to throw a party for them.

"About twenty-five of them turned up, so I put them in the trucks and took them to an inn up in the hills, a small hot-spring resort. We had to get out and push where it got too steep for those charcoal-burning things. But we made it eventually, and I rounded up all the geisha in the place.

"I'd taken along booze and cigarettes, sugar, blankets and other stuff, so they gave us a royal welcome. We had a whale of a time; two days we stayed. But then, while my back was turned, I found that all the trucks except one had disappeared. D'you know what had happened? My own fucking men had gone and stolen them! It meant there were thieves *everywhere*: you couldn't relax with anybody. Talk about biting the hand that feeds you!... So I told the rest of them to go to hell, and came away on my own in the last truck."

"Did you ever get the trucks back?" one of us asked him.

"Like hell I did! You didn't expect me to go cap in hand and report it to the police, did you? Anyway, by the time I got back to the base there wasn't a thing left. Nothing. It wasn't just the stuff in the warehouses, either: there weren't any *warehouses* any more. Roofs, walls, they'd stripped them clean. Not a telephone or power cable left. Not a telegraph pole. Even the underground cables had been dug up and had disappeared into thin air."

"And the stuff you swiped," I said, "it's still stashed away somewhere?"

"Yep. You name it, it's there."

"What kind of things?" I asked him. Cars, he said, engines, electric fans, sewing machines, sugar, alcohol, tin, sheets of steel, silk—it seems he'd even got an electrocardiograph, which you couldn't have found even in the best hospitals then. So I asked him if he couldn't show us some of it. Saburo looked as if that was just what he'd been waiting for, and he started bringing samples in. One thing that sticks in my mind is a bale of silk—thick, heavy stuff like damask, a yard wide and a hundred yards long. I'm not exaggerating. Pure silk.

Well, all good things come to an end. I heard later that he'd set himself up in business and made a packet. But, before long, someone put the finger on him, he was investigated by the occupation people, and all the stolen goods he still had left were confiscated, though he didn't get sent to jail.

But, you know, all the while he was telling us his story, he never looked sorry for himself. In fact, the worse things got, the more he laughed about it. He was a real character, he was....

Below Zero

It was just after I'd turned forty-seven, so it must have been 1951. The Korean war was going strong, and my new gambling place in Tokyo was doing really well. Early that spring, Osei suddenly turned up again, out of the blue. I was surprised, I can tell you—I mean, there hadn't been a word from her since she disappeared years ago.

"Osei!" I said. "What've you been up to?"

"I'm sorry," she answered, smiling. "Not even contacting you all this while."

"You had me worried. I didn't know what to do, I owe you money and—"

"Now, stop it," she said. "What's that between friends like us?"

"Well, anyway, it's good to see you."

And I took her through to the back room. She looked just as smart as always, but there was something foreign-looking about her this time. Her rings, and the things in her hair, the fastener on her sash—they didn't seem quite Japanese.

"What's brought you back here now?" I asked her when we'd settled down.

"I need somewhere to stay for a while," she said. She was always one for springing things on you like that. Whatever her reasons, though, I couldn't refuse, so I told her she could stay as long as she liked.

But it led to trouble in the end. I found out later that she was dealing in stimulants, and she'd come to Tokyo on business. From time to time, I'd see her taking cans or bottles of something into her room, but if I asked her what was in them she just wriggled out of it, said it wasn't important.

I, for one, wasn't going to press her if she preferred to keep it secret, but Okyo was really worried. She'd never much liked Osei.

"It's not that I mind you being soft on her," she said. "But no good's going to come of having her here."

"You don't need to get so burned up about it," I told her, trying to calm her down. "She'll be going back to Kobe before long."

But, to tell the truth, I was a bit scared myself as well. The guy who brought the stuff was just a kid—tall, about twenty, probably a student. "Good morning," he'd say, coming in with a big suitcase. "Sorry to barge in like this." Then Osei would disappear upstairs with him, and you wouldn't hear a sound from them for a couple of hours till the kid came clattering down the stairs again. "Thanks. See you," he'd say, and leave.

This began to put the wind up me, and I made up my mind to have it out with her. But she must have cottoned on, because one day she just cleared out, without a word, and never came back.

It was about a month and a half after she'd disappeared again that I got a summons from the police.

When I turned up at the station, I discovered it had to do with liquid amphetamine. I knew about the stuff, of course: Saburo—the guy I was just talking about—once brought a can of it to my place. When I asked him where he'd got hold of it, he said there'd been loads of it in the cellars of the navy hospital; apparently the kamikaze pilots had been using it to help them stay alert. He was selling it at ten yen an ampoule. But I told him to get lost: the old boss of the Dewaya, and Muramatsu too, had both been killed by drugs.

A steady flow of it had been coming onto the black market,

and it wasn't hard to find—at one stage they were even selling it openly at ordinary drugstores. And for a while after the war the number of addicts was a real problem. But in 1951 or 1952, the police began to crack down on it. Osei, according to the detective I spoke to, was known to be a dealer, and though they hadn't caught her or the carrier, they'd more or less worked out the route they'd been using.

"Look," the detective said, "do us a favor, will you? We know you don't handle the stuff yourself, but you're in for aiding and abetting. So why not just admit it? It won't count as a serious offense."

There was a lot more of the same spiel. Their methods may have changed since the war, but they were still bastards—poking their noses into everything you did. Anyway, it went to trial. I had two good lawyers—one had been a judge, the other a member of the Lower House—but, given my own statement and the police report, I was told I'd be lucky to get away with only a year in jail. So I decided to serve the sentence without appealing. I was out on bail at the time the sentence was first confirmed, and it wasn't until September 1953 that I actually went inside.

After keeping me for about a month in a Tokyo jail, they decided to send me and ten other men north to Hokkaido, to a prison at the far end of the island, across the strait from Russia. We went by train, then ferry, then train again; two days, it took.

The chief thing I remember about life in Abashiri is working in conditions that made you wonder how the *warders* could stand it. Unless the temperature went down to minus twenty-two, they kept us at it in the fields outside even in a gale or a blizzard. Then, when the snow really settled in and work in the fields became impossible, they sent us up into the hills to cut down timber. The snow made it much easier to tow the trees away. They were big, those trees—a good four feet across the trunk—and after hacking them down, we'd drive a couple of big spikes into the wood, fasten ropes to them and, with a yell at the horses, haul them off like sledges down the slopes.

Horses are amazing creatures. I mean, the strength they've got—the way they'd heave and heave at those great trees, with the steam rising off their backs, till they finally got them moving. You see, the trunks were heavy—several times heavier than in summer—because their bark was frozen. The heaviest of the lot were the yews, probably the best-quality wood available then, with a very close grain; they used to make pencils out of it. But it was *hard*, too: if you banged your head against it, it made you see stars, like being swiped with an iron bar.

Getting the roots up was the toughest job of all. Even the horses couldn't budge them if the trees had only just been felled. So they'd leave them for a year, then drive an iron thing with points like a rake into the stump, hitch five horses together, and tug it out. Later, they'd cut it up small and use it as fuel in the prison kitchens and the stoves.

It's funny, you know—while we were doing that kind of work, we'd forget all about being prisoners, we'd get so wrapped up in it. The men really put their backs into it, sweating like pigs, and whenever a great big stump suddenly tilted over and slipped out of the ground, their faces lit up like kids....

There was one prisoner in my cell that I remember well. Nagano Seiji, his name was.

Nagano told me he'd been a foreman at a building site in

Tokyo. One day, he got into an argument with one of the laborers; the other man pulled a knife, so Nagano whipped out a sword he'd got hidden away and sliced his right arm off at the shoulder.

"He died almost immediately—loss of blood," Nagano said. "I'd had some practice at it."

I asked him what he meant, and he said he'd cut off dozens of arms during the war.

"Come off it," I told him, "I don't believe it."

"Why not? And I'm not talking about enemy troops, either."

"You mean it was our *own* men?"

"That's right." He nodded and grinned. "Of course, they weren't *alive*...."

Well, I thought it was a lot of bullshit, and if it was a joke, it was a pretty sick one. But he wasn't kidding, as he explained.

He'd been in the attack on Hsüchou in March of the year after full-scale war had broken out between Japan and China. But his unit had been ambushed and as good as wiped out.

"We were about halfway across a field of wheat when suddenly we were caught in enemy crossfire—a real hail of bullets. The next thing we knew, the Chinese had withdrawn, but our company and platoon commanders had been killed, and when the corporal did a roll call, less than half the men answered. We'd lost forty men. Some of them were wounded and dying in the wheat.

"The corporal then said we should collect the dead together and burn them on the spot. But I told him there wasn't time; we were heavily outnumbered, and as soon as it got dark the enemy would probably counterattack. We'd *all* get wiped out.

" 'What d'you think we should do with them, then?' the

242

corporal said, in quite a state. 'Just leave them?'

" 'No, but there isn't time to burn as many bodies as this.'

" 'Then what about cutting off their heads and taking them with us?'

" 'They'd be too heavy.'

" 'We could carry fingers or arms,' he said.

" 'Fingers are no good. Let's take their arms.' "

So the two of them, Nagano told me, used swords on the dead bodies. No fancy stuff—they were in too much of a hurry; they just hacked off the arms at the shoulder, then tied them all together, dozens of them, and slung them on a pole. When they got back to somewhere safe, they burned them. The only problem was, they'd have to hand over the right ashes to the right families. So, as they were cutting off each arm, they'd tie a rag around it with the man's name on it; and later, when they laid them on the brushwood, one by one, the corporal wrote down the name in a notebook, before the things went up in smoke.

Nagano told me other stories about the war as well. There was nothing sentimental about *him*—it didn't bother him at all that some of his pals had been killed. He said he'd been given any number of decorations, and I expect it was true. Let's face it, it's men like him that make the best soldiers, isn't it?...

Anyway, a year passed in no time at all, and before long I was outside the gates meeting all the gang. But, for some reason or other, the train was delayed, and we missed the ferry across to the main island. I was furious; I'd wanted to get back to Asakusa as soon as possible. But it was dark by then, so we booked into an inn.

That was where we were lucky. We were pretty shaken the

243

next morning when we heard that the ferry we were supposed to have taken had sunk. It was the *Toya-maru* disaster. A
typhoon came that way unexpectedly, and more than a thousand people drowned. You never know your luck, do you?...

Old Acquaintance

Ijichi Eiji was sitting on the sofa, his head swaying slightly from side to side. A soft spring sunlight shone through the glass of the sliding doors.

"Isn't it time you lay down again?" said Hatsuyo.

"I'm all right. Bring in that thing I was telling you about, will you?" He lit a cigarette for himself and took a puff at it. The woman soon came back, holding a heavy-looking object wrapped in paper. She put it on the table and opened it, to reveal the black rock I'd already seen once before.

"I don't want it to be a nuisance, doctor," he said, "but I wonder if I could give you this." He squinted at it sleepily. "If you put it in the right kind of shallow dish and pour clean water over it, it looks quite impressive, especially in the morning light."

He poked lightly at the stone with a dry, brown finger, and it rocked a little in the sunlight.

On the way home, I stopped at a shop and bought a low, bluish-colored bowl of the right size. The following day, however, I had a cold and took to my bed. It continued for a week, and it still hadn't cleared up completely when one day, quite unexpectedly, a letter arrived. According to the postmark, it was from Ishioka, about twenty miles northeast of where I lived.

When I opened it, this is what it said:

> *It's turned a lot warmer, so I hope you're better by now. I want to thank you for all the nice talks we had this winter. I'd been thinking that I'd stay in Tsuchiura for the rest of my time, but I suddenly decided to move to Ishioka. My health is much the same as ever. There's a hospital near here where they said*

they'd send somebody over to have a look at me whenever there's anything wrong, so please don't worry about me. I'm sure you're as busy as ever, so take care of yourself.

Yours sincerely,

Ijichi Eiji

That was all. It was so sudden that I couldn't imagine what was behind it. I tried telephoning Hatsuyo, but she must have been away, because there was never any answer. So, once I'd recovered, I decided to go to Ishioka to find out for myself.

I had no trouble finding the place. It was a restaurant in the center of town, with a miniature wisteria stretching out its branches in a pot beside the entrance.

I asked for him at the cash register.

"Just a moment, sir," the girl said, and trotted off toward the kitchen. Almost at once, a rather refined-looking woman appeared.

She seemed to be in her mid-fifties, though she might have been older. She bowed and said, as though she'd known me for years: "You've been so good to him. I'm afraid his room's a bit cramped, but would you like to come upstairs?"

He was lying in an eight-mat room, with a flower arrangement in one corner.

"You shouldn't have come all this way just to see me," he said in a husky voice.

"How are you?" I asked.

"As you can see." He then introduced me to the woman, saying that she owned the restaurant, and was now looking after him.

She bowed to me again, her forehead touching the tatami this time. Returning the formality, I found myself wondering what her connection with the man was, but he made no move to enlighten me. He changed the subject by saying I'd lost a little weight, and nothing further was said about the matter. There seemed to be some phlegm stuck

246

in his throat, and with every breath he took there was a drawn-out wheezing sound.

"I haven't forgotten to water the stone as you told me to," I said.

"My old boss used to say it reminded him of Mt. Asama, but to me it looked just like one of the hills near our base in Korea.... Have you ever done any climbing, doctor?"

"I used to, but I'm a bit past it now."

"Don't be silly—you've hardly reached your prime!"

A grin passed over the dark, mottled cheeks, and he coughed moistly a couple of times. The woman brought a teapot and poured some fresh tea into my cup.

"Do you want some too?" she asked him.

"No, I'll have it later. When I drink tea," he explained to me, "I always have to take a leak; it's a nuisance. By the way—do you remember me talking about Saburo?"

"The man who made a pile at the end of the war?"

"That's right. He turned up suddenly just the other day. Five or six days ago, wasn't it?"

"Four," the woman put in.

"Was it?... Anyway, he hadn't changed a bit. The same funny little man with shifty-looking eyes. 'Nice to see you, boss,' he said, 'it's been a while. You're looking pretty well.' But he went straight on: 'To tell the truth, I heard a rumor you hadn't long to go, so I hopped on a train to see you one last time before you croaked.' And he roared with laughter, the little bastard. Then we got to talking, said what fun it'd been in the old days, when you could do more or less as you liked. Everybody's so serious nowadays, there's no fun in things at all. Anyway, I asked him what he's doing now, and it turns out he's got a job cleaning bars, snack bars—that sort of place. Not that he's ashamed of it—oh no. 'I like to do things properly,' he said. 'Once they've seen what I can do, they never ask anyone else. I do two places before lunch, and two more in the afternoon. Then I get on my bike* and go fishing. Or go to the races if I feel like it.' "

"So he hasn't changed much?"

"Just the same as ever. But he's getting on, too, like the rest of us. If you want to hear his story, you'd better hurry up."

"I would like to meet him, actually."

"I thought you might, so I got him to leave his phone number. If you're interested, I'll call him for you."

"I'd appreciate it. Still, it's more important to me that you get better. I haven't heard all you have to tell me yet."

"You mean you don't want me to die till you've heard the end of the story? You're more of a stickler than I thought, doctor. Actually, though, nothing much happened after I came back from Abashiri —nothing worth telling you about, at least. Well, there was one little incident that ended up with me cutting off another finger, but ..."

"When did it happen?"

"No, don't ask—honestly, it was a silly business.... Anyway," he went on, "Kamezo died soon after I got out, and I was getting a bit decrepit myself, so I decided to retire.... You must have thought at first that, being kind of well known in the yakuza world, I'd have some pretty exciting tales to tell. But, you know, the yakuza live on the shady side of life—it's not half as flashy as people think. I feel a bit bad about letting you come so often to that shack of mine, and not being able to tell you anything really interesting."

"Nonsense! You've no idea how much it's meant to me, getting to know you."

The woman put a little plate in front of me, with a cake in the shape of a nightingale on it.

"I don't know if you like sweet things, doctor...," she said.

"It's clever how they make them, isn't it?" I replied, looking at the cake admiringly.

"I went to Fukagawa yesterday," she said, "to the Tomioka Hachiman shrine. I bought them on the way back."

248

"Do you often go to Tokyo?"

"No, hardly ever."

She smiled and poured me another cup of tea.

"I remember, doctor," the man put in, "you had a picture in your place. Asakusa in the old days. They said your father did it. Is that right?"

"Yes. He didn't start painting till he was well into his sixties. That one was done when he was around seventy. And he's still working as a doctor, too."

"It's just like the Asakusa I knew when I was young. The slum area, with the wives squatting outside their shoddy little tenements, gossiping as they cooked some fish for supper on little charcoal grills.... The kids behind the shoji with their tattered paper.... And the men in cotton half-coats, walking home along the boards that covered the open drains.... When I worked at the coal depot, I used to see that kind of scene every day, but almost before I realized it, the whole thing had changed. Then, after I retired, I came to see you—and there was that picture. It really took me back.... Is it still there?"

"Oh yes."

"I'm glad."

It was past two o'clock by the time I called a halt to the conversation and, with a promise to come again soon, went back downstairs. The woman came out into the road to see me off. I was still completely in the dark as to who she was.

Ijichi Eiji died less than a month later. The funeral was a very quiet affair. I met Saburo there, and was astonished to find him exactly as Eiji had pictured him. I introduced myself, and he told me that Eiji had phoned him about me. "Come and look me up sometime," he said.

I also saw Hatsuyo at the funeral, for the first time in several months.

"How are you getting home?" I asked.

"Well, I came by train," she said, so I offered to take her in my car. This gave me a chance to ask her about the woman in Ishioka.

"That was Omitsu," she said. "The girl he ran off with all those years ago. Didn't he tell you?"

"Who'd have thought it.... I had the impression they never saw each other again."

"To be quite honest, I didn't know much about it myself. I only took up with him during the war, years later."

She glanced over at me as we drove along.

"So you'd never met her before?" I asked.

"When Kamezo died—it's quite a while ago now—she came to the wake.... I heard later that she'd had a rough time after that business with Eiji, but in the end she went back to the inn her parents ran, married a decent man who was adopted into the family, and kept the inn going after both her parents died. I expect Eiji knew about it, but he doesn't seem to have gone to see her. When Kamezo died, though, she turned up at the wake, alone. And it was only a few months later that he cut off the other finger."

"What did he do it for?"

"He went to visit her, and got into a quarrel there. It was all so stupid.... He just went out in the morning, and when he came home the finger was gone."

"It must have been quite a quarrel."

"If only it had been, I wouldn't have minded so much.... Anyway, after Kamezo's funeral he went over to her place, and found her alone. So they were sitting there chatting, just the two of them, when the husband got home. According to Eiji at least, the man seemed to be a bit peculiar. He'd checked up on her, and knew all the details.

"Anyway, Eiji introduced himself, and the husband—apparently he was fairly drunk—got Omitsu to bring them some more saké, then started rambling on about the past. Eiji felt a bit awkward and tried

250

to leave, but the other man wouldn't let him go. Before long, he'd got himself worked up and began to shout, laying into Eiji for showing up suddenly like that when he wasn't there."

"It took some guts to do that, knowing Eiji was a yakuza."

"I expect he thought his wife had cheated on him. And he wasn't sober, either. Anyway, he ended up punching Eiji."

"That bad, was it?"

"And you know what Eiji did then? Of all the stupid things—he went and cut his finger off—there, on the spot, the middle finger of his left hand. I ask you!"

"When was this?"

"He was over sixty-five at the time."

"Not so long ago, then."

"No, it wasn't. And just think of it—losing both fingers for the same thing! I suppose he wanted to make himself look good in front of Omitsu. I mean, no yakuza's going to do that just to save some little innkeeper's skin—a lousy small-town drunk like that. But Eiji—no, he has to chop it straight off for his old flame's sake. Just to impress her."

She gave a faint, ironic smile and lit a cigarette. On both sides of the road, paddy fields swept past, and the sunset still lingered in the sky beyond the hills.

"And what happened then?"

"She left home. Eiji made various arrangements to help her get by, and then—I'm not sure, but I think he bought her the restaurant she's got now."

"I see...."

"I suppose you're wondering why he didn't move in with her right away," she said, looking over at me.

"Well, I can't help being curious."

"I know you can't, and I'm not blaming you. But don't forget, I may not be much to look at now, but I'm still a woman, and I've got *my pride.*" She spoke rather more strongly than usual.

"Around the time I first went to live with him, I wasn't well and couldn't do anything much. Okyo used to do all the work by herself. Even so, once Okyo had set up in business on her own, I ran the household. And for a long time after that, I looked after him myself. It may have been because of that—maybe he felt he couldn't just throw me out. And besides, we had a daughter; I expect that was another reason, too.

"We came to Tsuchiura in the first place because our daughter took up with a man there; they said there was a nice house near them, and couldn't we join them, so we decided to move. Unfortunately, she fell out with the man and went back to Tokyo—she's got a place of her own now, where she teaches Japanese dancing. Anyway, the two of us were left there by ourselves. But now that I knew about Omitsu, I was forever wondering whether I shouldn't give him up. Of course, I'd always rather be with somebody than live alone, even if the other person's sick. But I couldn't help brooding about it, and I began to think it was cruel in a way to keep him with me. And in the end it got too much for me.

"So one day I went to Ishioka and put it to her. Yes, she said, she'd like to take him, if it was all right with me. So I said, well then, I'll make you a present of him, and that settled it.

"But you know, I never meant to keep him till he got that feeble. By the time out daughter went back to Tokyo, I'd already made up my mind. It was your fault, doctor, that it got so late."

She struck a match, without taking her eyes off the dark road ahead.

"I thought his talks with you would be over in no time. But then you started coming almost every day—all through the winter, too. In his heart of hearts, I imagine he wanted to be with her as soon as possible. But he wanted to talk, as well.... So it was put off, and put off, and then his health broke down. If anybody, it should be you, doctor,

252

that Omitsu resents, not me."

"I had no idea...."

"Don't worry—I wasn't really serious. If he'd really wanted to go, he wouldn't have waited a single day, even. It wasn't anyone's fault, really, that he left it so late."

Outside the car windows, the lights of Tsuchiura were already flicking by.

"Incidentally," said Hatsuyo, "there's one last thing I'd like to ask you. What do you really feel about him? I mean, he had a pretty wild life, and he killed a man, whatever his reasons, and he went to jail several times. It was a rotten world he lived in. Maybe that's what made him interesting for you. But you went on seeing him, for months on end. Why?"

"Well.... You know, you were too close to him; that's why you can say things like that. It may take a while, but you'll see him differently then."

"Really?..."

"I promise you."

"All right, I'll take your word for it.... Could you drop me off at the station, please? You see, I've moved in with my daughter in Tokyo. Why don't you come and visit us sometime—when the morning-glory fair is on, for instance?"

As she was getting out of the car, she wrote down her address and phone number on a scrap of paper.

"Well, then—goodbye, doctor."

"Goodbye."

And she went off slowly up the station stairs.

英文版 浅草博徒一代
CONFESSIONS OF A YAKUZA

1995 年 4 月30日　第 1 刷発行
2003 年 8 月 1 日　第11刷発行

著　者　佐賀　純一

訳　者　ジョン・ベスター

発行者　畑野文夫

発行所　講談社インターナショナル株式会社
　　　　〒112-8652 東京都文京区音羽 1-17-14
　　　　電話　03-3944-6493 (編集部)
　　　　　　　03-3944-6492 (営業部・業務部)
　　　　ホームページ　www.kodansha-intl.co.jp

印刷所　株式会社 平河工業社

製本所　株式会社 フォーネット社

DISCOVER JAPAN Words, Customs, and Concepts

The Japan Culture Institute

Short, practical descriptions of the words, ideas and customs of Japan.

"The one book you must have if you're heading for Japan..."—*Essex Journal*

Volume 1
Paperback: 216 pages, 110 x 182 mm, b/w photos, ISBN 0-87011-835-8
Volume 2
Paperback: 224 pages, 110 x 182 mm, b/w photos, ISBN 0-87011-836-6

THE ANATOMY OF DEPENDENCE

Takeo Doi, MD. Translated by John Bester

The classic analysis of *amae*, the indulging, passive love which supports an individual within a group, and a key concept in Japanese psychology.

"Profound insights not only into the character of Japan but into the nuances of dependency relationships."—Ezra Vogel

Paperback: 184 pages, 110 x 182 mm, ISBN 0-87011-494-8

THE ANATOMY OF SELF The Individual Versus Society

Takeo Doi, MD. Translated by Mark A. Harbison

A fascinating exploration of the role of the individual in Japan, and Japanese concepts of self-awareness, communication, and relationships.

"An excellent book."—Frank A. Johnson, MD., U.C. San Francisco

Paperback: 176 pages, 110 x 182 mm, ISBN 0-87011-902-8

APPRECIATIONS OF JAPANESE CULTURE

Donald Keene

The dean of Japanese studies provides a classic introduction to the beauties and intricacies of Japanese literature, offering an essential companion to the study of Japanese prose and poetry of all eras.

Paperback: 350 pages, 110 x 182 mm, ISBN 4-7700-0956-9

ON FAMILIAR TERMS A Journey Across Cultures

Donald Keene

The intimate and engaging memoirs of the renowned scholar and translator who "discovered" modern Japanese literature.

Paperback: 306 pages, 142 x 213 mm, ISBN 1-56836-129-7

PUBLIC PEOPLE, PRIVATE PEOPLE
Portraits of Some Japanese

Donald Richie

The private recollections of long-time Japan resident Donald Richie capture the personalities of certain Japanese people—some famous, some unknown—with insight, humor, and elegance.
"His portraits are unforgettable."—Tom Wolfe

Paperback: 212 pages, 110 x 182 mm, ISBN 4-7700-2104-6
Previously published as: *Some Japanese Portraits,* and *Geisha, Gangster, Neighbor, Nun*

THE ESSENCE OF ZEN
Dharma Talks Given in Europe and America

Sekkei Harada

An informal introduction to the fundamentals of Buddhist thought and the principles of Zen practice from one of the foremost Zen masters in Japan, specifically tailored for audiences in Europe and the United States.

Hardcover: 200 pages, 128 x 188 mm, ISBN 4-7700-2199-2

THE BOOK OF TEA

Kakuzo Okakura
Foreword and Afterword by Soshitsu Sen XV, Grand Tea Master, Urasenke School of Tea

The seminal text on the meaning and practice of tea. Written 80 years ago, the book is less about tea than it is about the philosophical and aesthetic traditions basic to Japanese culture.

Paperback: 160 pages, 110 x 182 mm, 8 B/W photos, ISBN 4-7700-1542-9

THE TEA CEREMONY New Edition

Sen'o Tanaka
Foreword by Edwin O. Reischauer   Preface by Yasushi Inoue

A comprehensive look at the sources and inspiration of an ancient discipline by one of Japan's contemporary tea masters. Sen'o Tanaka traces the practice from its earliest origins to the present day, and examines in detail the individuals who helped it evolve.

Hardcover: 224 pages, 189 x 257 mm, 50 color plates,
50 b/w photos, 50 line drawings; glossary; index, ISBN 4-7700-2125-9

THE JAPANESE THROUGH AMERICAN EYES

Sheila K. Johnson

Anthropologist Sheila Johnson looks into the images and stereotypes of Japanese produced by American popular culture. A revealing look at movies, war propaganda, cartoons, and best-selling novels.

Paperback: 208 pages, 110 x 182 mm, ISBN 4-7700-1450-3, Territories: Japan only

BLUEPRINT FOR A NEW JAPAN
The Rethinking of a Nation

Ichiro Ozawa   Introduction by Sen. Jay Rockefeller

Political pundit Ozawa outlines the steps Japan must take to become a "normal" nation in the post-Cold War world.
"Nobody trying to understand Japan can afford to ignore this book."
—The Economist

Hardcover: 208 pages, 152 x 226 mm, ISBN 4-7700-1871-1
Paperback: 208 pages, 110 x 182 mm, ISBN 4-7700-2041-4
Territories: PB Japan only

THE THIRD CENTURY

Joel Kotkin & Yoriko Kishimoto

As the U.S. enters its third century it faces serious competition from Asia, but, the authors argue, it can withstand the challenge by adopting a realistic and resilient attitude.

Paperback: 304 pages, 110 x 182 mm, ISBN 4-7700-1452-X, Territories: Japan only

BLINDSIDE
Why Japan is Still on Track to Overtake the U.S. by the Year 2000

Eamonn Fingleton

"A book of fundamental originality and importance...Those who read it now will be ahead of the game." —James Fallows
"A brilliant book full of fresh insights that explode carefully nurtured myths about Japan, as well as much conventional wisdom." —Clyde Prestowitz

Paperback: 410 pages, 128 x 188 mm, ISBN 4-7700-2146-1, Territories: Japan only

ABOUT FACE
How I Stumbled onto Japan's Social Revolution

Clayton Naff

This unique analysis based on the personal and professional experiences of an American journalist reveals the changes occurring in the Japanese home and in the working world.
"The best guide to the internal pressures on Japan to change." — Chalmers Johnson

Paperback: 352 pages, 140 x 210 mm, notes, index, ISBN 1-56836-131-9

STRAITJACKET SOCIETY
An Insider's Irreverent View of Bureaucratic Japan

Masao Miyamoto   Foreword by Juzo Itami

A well-placed insider, Dr. Miyamoto presents a valuable and frank critique of the "closed society" of the Japanese bureaucracy. "Miyamoto has lifted the veil on Japan's powerful but oblique bureaucracy."—*Los Angeles Times*

Hardcover: 200 pages, 152 x 226 mm, ISBN 4-7700-1848-7
Paperback: 200 pages, 113 x 182 mm, ISBN 4-7700-1995-5

EDUCATING ANDY
The Experience of a Foreign Family in the Japanese Elementary School System

Anne & Andy Conduit

Both insightful and humorous, this insider's view of the Japanese school system from the perspective of a blond, blue-eyed, twelve-year-old paints a revealing portrait of the Japanese character.

Paperback: 224 pages, 110 x 182 mm, b/w photos, ISBN 4-7700-1921-1

JAPAN FOR STARTERS
52 Things You Need to Know About Japan

Charles Danziger

Fifty-two sketches introduce the fundamentals of Japan's modern, traditional, and business worlds. Combining a hard-earned insider's knowledge with an irrepressible sense of fun, *Japan for Starters* is insightful, informative, and humorous—a delight to read.

Paperback: 174 pages, 110 x 182 mm, line drawings, ISBN 4-7700-2087-2
Previously published as *The American Who Couldn't Say Noh*.

WOMANSWORD
What Japanese Words Say About Women

Kittredge Cherry

Valuable insights into women's roles in Japan, their relations with men, and their view of themselves. An informal glossary with brief essays that collectively describe Japanese womanhood.

Paperback: 160 pages, 110 x 182 mm, ISBN 4-7700-1655-7

WORDS IN CONTEXT

Takao Suzuki   Translated by Akira Miura

One of Japan's foremost linguists offers a provocative analysis of the complex relationship between language and culture, psychology and lifestyle.

Paperback: 180 pages, 110 x 182 mm, 14 line illustrations, ISBN 0-87011-642-8

MANGA! MANGA! The World of Japanese Comics

Frederick L. Schodt   Introduction by Osamu Tezuka

Profusely illustrated with the most representative examples of the genre, this is the first book in English to explore the world of Japanese comics.

Paperback: 260 pages, 182 x 257 mm, 8 color pages, 185 b/w photos, 96 pages of comics stories, ISBN 0-87011-752-1

A FAR VALLEY   Four Years in a Japanese Village

Brian Moeran

An intimate portrayal of the rhythms of life in a rural community in a remote valley in southern Japan, masterfully captured through the joyful and tragic experiences of anthropologist Moeran and his family. "An honest and personal odyssey."—Alan Booth, author of *Looking for the Lost*
"This is the very best kind of book"—Richard Bowring, Cambridge University

Paperback: 264 pages, 140 x 210 mm, ISBN 4-7700-2301-4
Previously published as *Okubo Diary*.

NEIGHBORHOOD TOKYO

Theodore C. Bestor

This highly readable anthropological study of a small, urban neighborhood provides insights into the whole social structure of modern Japan.

Paperback: 368 pages, 110 x 182 mm, ISBN 4-7700-1496-1, Territories: Japan only

THE HIDDEN ORDER
Tokyo Through the Twentieth Century

Yoshinobu Ashihara   Translated by Lynne E. Riggs

Using architecture as a metaphor for culture, renowned Japanese architect Yoshinobu Ashihara offers an insider's look at the apparent chaos of Tokyo.

Hardcover: 160 pages, 150 x 220 mm, 100 b/w photos and illustrations, ISBN 0-87011-912-5,
Paperback: 160 pages, 110 x 182 mm, 100 b/w photos and illustrations, ISBN 4-7700-1664-6

THE COMPACT CULTURE
The Japanese Tradition of "Smaller is Better"

O-Young Lee   Translated by Robert N. Huey

A provocative study of Japan's tendency to make the most out of miniaturization—a study of a philosophy of living that reveals the essence of Japanese character.

Paperback: 196 pages, 110 x 182 mm, 23 b/w illustrations, ISBN 4-7700-1643-3

LITERATURE/FICTION

Abe, Kobo	**THE FACE OF ANOTHER** **THE RUINED MAP** **SECRET RENDEZVOUS**
Agawa, Hiroyuki	**CITADEL IN SPRING** **THE RELUCTANT ADMIRAL**
Ariyoshi, Sawako	**THE DOCTOR'S WIFE** **KABUKI DANCER** **THE RIVER KI**
Boehm, Deborah	**A ZEN ROMANCE**
Booth, Alan	**LOOKING FOR THE LOST** **THE ROADS TO SATA**
Dazai, Osamu	**BLUE BAMBOO** **SELF PORTRAITS**
Enchi, Fumiko	**THE WAITING YEARS**
Endo, Shusaku	**THE SAMURAI** **SILENCE**
Hamill, Pete	**TOKYO SKETCHES**
Ibuse, Masuji	**BLACK RAIN** **CASTAWAYS** **SALAMANDER** **WAVES**
Ikenami, Shotaro	**THE MASTER ASSASSIN** **BRIDGE OF DARKNESS**
Ikezawa, Natsuki	**STILL LIVES**
Inoue, Yasushi	**LOU-LAN** **TUN-HUANG**
Ishikawa, Yoshimi	**STRAWBERRY ROAD**
Kaiko, Takeshi	**INTO A BLACK SUN**
Kawabata, Yasunari	**HOUSE OF THE SLEEPING BEAUTIES** **THE LAKE** **THE TALE OF THE BAMBOO CUTTER**
Kita, Morio	**GHOSTS**
Kizaki, Satoko	**THE PHOENIX TREE** **THE SUNKEN TEMPLE**
Komatsu, Sakyo	**JAPAN SINKS**
Kuroyanagi, Tetsuko	**TOTTO-CHAN**
Maruya, Saiichi	**A MATURE WOMAN** **RAIN IN THE WIND** **SINGULAR REBELLION**
Matsumoto, Seicho	**POINTS AND LINES** **THE VOICE**